Women
Challenge
the Lie

May 2017
Sharleen —
Let's celebrate together,
the Grace of Being Woman.
Big Love,
Shirlyn
Trudeau

Other Books by Regina Sara Ryan

Wellness Workbook, How to Achieve Enduring Health and Vitality, with John W. Travis, M.D.

Simply Well: Choices for a Healthy Life, with John W. Travis, M.D.

After Surgery, Illness or Trauma: 10 Steps to Renewed Energy and Health

No Child in My Life

Everywoman's Book of Common Wisdom, with Erica Jen and Lalitha Thomas

The Woman Awake, Feminine Wisdom for Spiritual Life

Praying Dangerously: Radical Reliance on God

Only God: A Biography of Yogi Ramsuratkumar

Breastfeeding, Your Priceless Gift to Your Baby and Yourself

Igniting the Inner Life

Stand Up, The Courage to Care, with Elyse April

Women Challenge the Lie

8 Radical Moves to Get Beyond "Never Good Enough"

Regina Sara Ryan & Shinay Tredeau

HOHM PRESS
Chino Valley, Arizona

Cover Design: Adi Zuccarello, adizuccarello.com

Interior Design and Layout: Becky Fulker, Kubera Book Design, Prescott, Arizona

ISBN: 978-1-942493-23-5

Hohm Press
P.O. Box 4410
Chino Valley, AZ 86323
800-381-2700
http://www.hohmpress.com

This book was printed in the U.S.A. on recycled, acid-free paper using soy ink.

For Lee, who gave me a big YES! when I asked his blessing in writing a book called *Stop Self Hatred*. This is that book.

– Regina

For the Women – Mothers, Sisters, Teachers, Friends, because with you I remember who I really am. And for the men who support us in becoming Woman.

– Shinay

Contents

Over time, my mind got quieter and something else happened. I began to feel into how Kali was slowly and ceaselessly showing me a new way of being. She was showing me a new way of thinking about myself. She showed me a way of knowing who I truly was/am underneath the life-long habit of negative thoughts. She overwhelmed my mind with the beauty of the divine feminine. She overwhelmed me with beauty. She showed me that every woman was *Her* and every woman was beautiful and loved. I was too. I was not left out of that generalization. She showed me over and over how to allow my negative self-image to be replaced by an authentic, positive self-regard and self-love. Not a surface assertion of "I'm beautiful" or "I'm a goddess," but a wild, unfettered understanding of my true nature. Every bit of me is loved and every bit of me is Her.

– Aditi Devi, *In Praise of Adya Kali*

Introduction

Shinay and I are friends – she at 29, me at 71. I've known her since she was born. One summer, when she was nine months old, I carried her for seven weeks through Europe, visiting England, France, and Germany with her parents and a ragtag entourage led by my spiritual teacher. She and I have been holding onto one another regularly ever since.

When Shinay went through undergraduate school at Prescott College, majoring in writing and dance, I was one of her mentors. Today, she is my yoga teacher and I am her writing coach. But more, we are friends. This book is a testimony to our twenty-nine-year love. We help each other – reminding each other of our intrinsic goodness. We work together whenever possible on projects of mutual interest. This book was conceived as a way to deepen our friendship and to continue to deal with the insanity of our minds' default button, the one that reads *never good enough*.

We know that so many of our age-peer friends – Shinay's in their late teens, twenties and thirties, mine in their fifties, sixties and seventies – have a similar default. Our friends aren't losers…far from it. They are talented artists with beautiful intentions; caring moms or grandmas or beloved partners, each with a loving heart and generous hands. Still, they undermine themselves. They find it hard to receive the love that is offered to them, or to look at and accept the mirrored reflections of profound goodness that we and others are reflecting for them. They've bought into the lie of *not quite (or never) good enough*. They can't quite believe they are deserving of love…yet. They don't walk around inside the reality of their own love, or the Great Love, but stay focused on seeking clues from the outside world to affirm that they just *might* be okay.

Our friends suffer, same as us. They carry weighty burdens that are hard to put down – burdens built from years of self-doubt, negativity, and skewed perceptions. Shinay and I wonder how so many of us learned these lies of *never good enough*. From our early family circumstances? From TV caricatures? From school peers? Maybe some chemical of self-loathing was added to the county water system. Certainly these events may reinforce that lie. But, the bottom line of it all?

We all come in as helpless babies, which brings with it certain obvious drawbacks, like ignorance and the need for survival. Until we grow up – until our eyes are fully opened, in the deepest sense of the term – ignorance and the necessity for survival will continue to run the show, obscuring our view of reality. Sadly, some of us never grow up.

From wherever or however these lies originated, we've adopted them as real, living as if they were true of us. We have sentenced ourselves to a small, tight view, often held ourselves back from risks (out of fear for survival), denied our basic goodness – and our "goddess"– and painfully endured a consistent drain of precious life force as we've struggled to keep the wolf from the door.

Comparisons with others, standards of unreachable perfection, and negative judgments about myself rob me (Regina) of energy and siphon off my creative juices. It's no wonder that I want to quit some important task or responsibility I've taken on; it's no wonder that I often find myself resistant to ever starting at all. I confront these "mind mosquitoes" (as my spiritual teacher used to call them) at my writing desk, and elsewhere. Shinay deals with them on her yoga mat amidst the hundreds of daily tasks she has committed to do. We suffer, within and for ourselves, and we suffer that our friends and sisters throughout the world suffer this type of limitation, too.

Determining to write this book was a way to declare that we recognized the lies and were ready to send them packing. *Enough!* we each said, alone and to one another. *Enough of never good enough!* we shout now together. Having an ally in this process of meeting the mosquitoes (or the monsters, which sometimes they are) is invaluable. Two is better than one when it comes to making a bigger noise.

This book is our invitation to you to make a similar declaration…for yourself; to make a joyful noise *with* us, and *for* and *with* women everywhere.

"When one flower opens, a hundred flowers open," says the poet Kabir.

What a wondrous garden that would make!

Ella's Declaration

Basic goodness is what flows up my spine; it keeps me upright, even when I can't sit straight. [Ella is physically handicapped.] It isn't about *me*, it's about that force that lives things. It's a green force. The life force. And *it* is good, as bad as things can get. Self-hatred, on the other hand, is a bunch of made-up conclusions, made up by a sick and demented view of stuff. It isn't true. Doesn't much matter who or what started it all, it's not real. It's just ideas, stories. That's why I'm all for laughing and exaggeration and silliness…and even cursing. It's good for me, and for you too.

WHY RADICAL MOVES?

This book is about radical moves, but generally not in the way that term is commonly used today, as in "fiercely unusual" or "extreme." That kind of radical move can be exhilarating, valuable, like a slap in the face to the status quo, or a surprise attack on conventional behavior. It might entail a leap across a chasm, or a leap into flight – like the great Baryshnikov made on an ordinary day, leaving his audiences stunned and even breathless.

But radical moves of that sort are more often short-lived, like protest marches or detox programs. They shock, or trouble, or generate immediate energy that is needed to leap an octave, but they don't (*they can't*) last forever. They rarely have staying power. Otherwise, they would cease to be radical, soon losing their front-page appeal...*Oh ah,* [yawn] *there goes another one!*

Some of this book is flavored with the spices that characterize such fierce or uncommon radical moves: like when we suggest that you take a powerful stand on behalf of yourself in the face of the lies you've been fed. That's radical! A bit of this book *is* about a radical confrontation of the holdouts, the hold-ups, the strangleholds you've agreed to, and the need for some practiced choreography or plain magic to assist you in breaking these grips. Yes, that's here, too. But that's only a part of what the term "radical moves" means for us.

The dictionary's first definition of "radical," and the one that underlies everything we'll develop here – the one we'll come back to repeatedly throughout this handbook – is this: "arising from or going to a root or source...something basic." We're in the *back-to-basics* business here. And we understand that *back to basics* is a problem for some, and a mystery to nearly everyone. Courage! We're with you.

You've picked up this book for a reason, or your sister-friend or mother (or male friend, husband or dad) handed it to you for a reason. Our guess is that *you want out* of this endless cycle of self-doubt and hatred. You know the price you pay for it. Yes? Well, maybe not. Maybe you don't fully get how costly this habit is yet, which is why the "price" will be one of the basics we will cover.

When you do appreciate how expensive this habit is, you'll start to look at it a bit differently.

If you're like most of us, that root or source or basic ground – the basic love, the basic goodness, the basic *Who Am I?* – generally eludes you. Maybe, like so many of us, you still circle the holy shrine of your own beauty and goodness again and again, but don't stop long enough to enter in. Maybe you refuse to believe that the shrine holds any mystery or power. Perhaps you don't want to admit how lost or frustrated or confused you feel.

Some of our friends are unwilling to consider going "to the source" because it seems connected somehow to religion, and the "spiritualized" people who talk about such things, and supposedly live there, aren't such sterling examples of whatever we imagine "source" should be, or would reveal. Maybe, like them, you're already jaded by the whole deal, thinking you've "been there, done that," and it didn't change anything. Or maybe you're simply afraid, or feel the need for a guide so as not to get lost in there. Maybe you think you've never even started on your real pilgrimage to the source and now you're too old for the hike.

"Radical moves" as we present them here are not necessarily dangerous, except to some tired old view of yourself. But don't underestimate how strong these tired old views can be! These radical moves don't necessarily require huge energy reserves. The moves that will be offered here are less about *doing something* and more about *being in relationship*…with yourself and with others.

Wanna play?

The Invitation

Consider this book a phone call from us. Okay, a text message if you wish. "Wanna walk? Wanna talk? Wanna play?" Shinay and I, and a select circle of your other sisters (some of whom you haven't even met yet), need you to help us find our way back to the source, back to the original innocence of our precious and inherent dignity, back to the tender soil of our feminine potency. We aren't here to offer an alternative to your present religious faith, or any new psychology or therapy. We're here to remind you – and ourselves – of what we are and always were. Of what we knew; where we were planted; and how to get ourselves back to that garden.

We (your new and old friends) assert that when we know ourselves as Woman, not just as "a woman," we don't give credence to self-diminishment.

But how to know this Woman with the capital W?

"You learn what Woman is by hanging out with other women," a wise teacher once told us. But there was a caveat here. The "hanging out" needed to get beyond the *blah blah blah*. Women together could simply continue to reinforce their own neuroses, fears, insecurities…and you've probably felt this. After spending time with another woman, you have sometimes felt drained rather than renewed. Complaint, blame, refusal to admit the new, the possible, is such a drag to be around. Boring at best, illness-producing at worst.

This book is our contribution to the cause of knowing Woman…and we will begin by establishing ourselves together, with you, beyond the *blah blah blah*. While you can read this book in solitary company, and while it is true that each of us must make this journey to source on her own…still, good company is one of the most valuable resources on the planet, and nobody but a fool attempts to make the ascent of Everest without support. Shinay and I have found so much more traction on the trail when we've been able to share the possibilities and pitfalls of this walk, this exploration.

Ideally, therefore, we urge you to meet up with another woman-friend (or several, if possible) to walk, to talk, to play this book together. Team up for the trek. Destination: source! As you establish a common ground of vulnerability and willingness to risk, the comparisons and doubts that might seem to assail you alone, or you more than others, will be revealed for what they are. Lies! Together, it is easier to face fears. Together, it is easier to spark a playful spirit that might lead you to dance or sing or paint or write or cook a great meal. To take a day trip or make a long, silent weekend retreat or engage whatever form of nurturing art you've been neglecting but you know can leave you truly delighted. This accessing of *the love you are* requires some hard work, as it can involve turning around habits of a lifetime. Hence, it is greatly to your advantage to undertake it in good company. To have a friend, a guide, a sister.

We believe that our life depends on getting beyond the self-hatred and the *blah blah blah* that keeps women isolated and disempowered. Our lives, your life – physically, emotionally, creatively, romantically, spiritually, relationally, clearly, cleanly, messily – depends on remembering Woman, nurturing yourself at source, and acknowledging and honoring others in their journey of remembrance. Haven't you had enough forgetfulness, enough self-hatred, self-doubt, never-good-enoughness, playing small, to last you for years? For decades?

Get ready to make a few radical moves!

OUR APPROACH

Delight

When Shinay and I started this project, we packed food for the day and headed for the Grand Canyon, which is less than two hours from our town. We hiked. We picnicked. We did yoga on the edge. We wrote poetry and sat in silent amazement! We agreed to have a good time, and we did, which didn't mean that all was easy or peaceful. At times, then and throughout this process, we've hit some tough places where we endured misunderstanding, and shared fears and tears.

On numerous occasions we met in a favorite coffee shop, reading what we'd written, making plans, reporting on the experiments we tried and the conversations we had with other women about the subject. A few times we invited other women-friends to meet with us, a sort of tea party of remarkable sisters dedicated to self-remembrance.

Late one summer we spent a day by the Verde River that winds through Oak Creek Canyon, near Sedona. We didn't write on that day at all. We swam and sat silently in the rushing water. We simply fed our souls.

We were convinced that unless delight kissed this process we were doomed to drop it. But our delight was broad-based – not just some bubble-bath giggly-girl delight. We found delight in the sweat of working the program, of putting aside the time and spaces that allowed the book to birth; we found delight in the fine art of making distinctions and articulating our visions, our aims. And we attempted to design a book that would bring delight to our readers – to you and your friends – as you all engaged what might be…would likely be…a significant effort.

Time

Each of the topic essays that follows might be used for a month of reflections, writings, meetings: eight radical moves in eight months, with time off for holidays and vacations. Carrying one topic on for any longer than eight months, you might get tired of the point being made. Any less, you might not give yourself the chance to really explore and talk and play about whatever you need to walk, talk or play about. (Whatever you do, have fun!)

This program takes time. We didn't rush writing it, and we hope you'll give yourself the time to do it, and enjoy it. Like us, you've been working the Self-Undermining Program for a long time. You've got some strong habits and some heavy self-defeating dialogues at play in your psyche. Give yourself the time to build a new workout routine – to enroll some new habits. Take one radical move at a time. Work it. Write about it. Share the results of your experiments. Tell the bottom-line truth to yourself (and your friend/support team) about what you know and can do, and what you don't know and can't do...yet. Be gentle. Be forgiving. Be imperfect. (We mean it!) Take time.

In Stages

This process of disavowing *never good enough* reveals itself in various phases or stages. We start with awareness, becoming familiar with the consistency of the lie and how deeply we've bought into it; we see our patterns of self-hatred. Then we bring in forgiveness, which softens the edges around ourselves, allowing us to relax and give ourselves permission, space, caring. (Call it compassion, which is precisely what it is.) Then, as we slowly ease into the recognition and the forgiveness/softening, we exert the courage to persevere for the long haul, because we know that change doesn't happen overnight. Finally (if there is a "final" anything), we open to life in its multifaceted wonder – to life beyond the lie.

These four stages will not be spelled out explicitly within each chapter, but they form the matrix for the whole structure. Awareness, forgiveness and softening, courage and perseverance, and opening will underlie every move we suggest. Unless we can see clearly what *isn't* happening and tell the truth about *what is* – like how pervasive our self-hating programs have become (the stage of becoming aware) – we stay in denial and confusion. Self-observation, meditation, writing, keeping lists…these are all methods that may help you to come to this honest assessment and motivate further conversation with your friends that will build new pathways in your brain and in your daily walks and works.

In the stage of forgiveness and softening, we understand that it is easy to recommend such methods to those we love. Don't you advise your sisters to forgive and take it easy when you see how rigid and unyielding they have become in their judgments and attitudes toward themselves? But will we do this toward ourselves? Not so easy. In this regard, we will be coaching you in the use of breath and body attention, exercise and movement, and in other ways to encourage this loosening up, this softening.

The next phase asks for courage and perseverance, and that is why a friend, a team, or a wise mentor can be invaluable on the journey. Ultimately, we must each build a reservoir of bravery to face the paradox that life is not a "crystal stair," or a straight-line affair. We will each be challenged to hoist the burden of our own gloriously imperfect selves, full of both wonder and wounds; to intelligently adjust this weight on our shoulders, like a backpack that we would rather jettison but which we know contains the tools for our survival; to make peace with the load that comes with being human; and to move forward (the phase of opening) with gratitude and curiosity at the privilege of being alive, ready and willing to see/hear/feel/ move in a new way – which really means to *love* in a new way.

The Sequence

These 8 Radical Moves and the reflections and questions we offer in these pages arose from years of work on self and from our conversations and interviews with other women. These 8 are not in some rigid order, or even in the order in which we learned them together. So if you skip one or two and get enthralled by others, you're still a good person. Never fear! Break the rules. Follow your interest and passion.

On the other hand, there is a sequence that may prove useful here. Our approach has been to start with some external moves and then to gently encourage deeper inner explorations. We introduce some general moves, and then invite you to get down to specifics. Some of you will find this sequencing to be useful in your work together. Carry on with our blessing.

Truth be told, you only need one access route to the heart of the heart, where love abides. We offer 8 (plus a bonus) because we are all so different. Some of us are mental types, others are emotional types, still others are moving types. We also offer 8 because one move sometimes gets boring and no longer encourages us forward.

Each of these Radical Moves, taken and practiced with regularity, actually has the potential of spiraling to the source, deepening and expanding the chasm of love for a lifetime. Find one or many that work for you and your close ones.

YOU WRITE THE BOOK, TOO

The first draft of this book came in the form of a novel, and has obviously changed radically since Shinay joined my team.

I (Regina) initially set out to tell a fictional story of a group of women (each character loosely based on one of my well-known friends) who find each other, tell their stories, and discover that each is plagued with self-doubt or self-loathing and is working with her tendency in some interesting or unique way. After meeting together for a year, these novel characters decide to write a book that might inspire other women to try out their methods. The second half of my early "novel" became the handbook written by this dedicated group.

As, with Shinay's help, that first book took on a whole new life, we recognized that many other books about overcoming self-hatred had already been and were continuing to be written all over the world. Single women, loving couples, teams of married women, bonded families of women, women with a common aim or a common religious faith were already coming together for one purpose: to remember who they are as Woman, in the presence of one another. They were meeting to reignite the sense of self-congruence and to reach out to others who shared this longing but couldn't quite give it a name yet. They were *doing* the book that we (Shinay and Regina) were merely writing down. We felt close to women around the world who were dealing together with this epidemic understatement of self-worth. We recognized that they might need only a tiny bit of alignment, a way to fulfill on a promise, and some handholding and tear-wiping in order to move from forgetfulness to remembrance. They might need a fearless editor to help them establish a real deadline for *their* book's appearance.

That could be our job — so we've declared it: to serve you and others who may be floundering in the means without a clear focus yet on the end. That is our job: to witness in our own struggles and joys to the satisfaction and empowerment that may be only a turn of a page away, and to encourage one and all, singly or in groups, to "write" their own handbooks, with or without words on paper, and identify their Radical Moves for moving beyond the blah blah blah and facing the lie that they are never good enough.

Together, we are offering *Women Challenge the Lie* as our contribution to bringing Woman alive in ourselves and in you. You decide if using *our* suggestions can serve you. You are already in the process, know it or not, and we encourage you to remember that. Build on what already is, and let's make – or continue to make – some Radical Moves together.

THANKS FOR STARTING

Thank you for buying or borrowing our book. Thanks even more for using our book. Thanks beyond measure for getting together with another friend or a group of women and becoming your own Woman-team or Woman-circle.

May you find courage, strength, and joy in the journey ahead.

We know these Radical Moves are useful because they continue to work for us. Some of these ideas are more powerful than others. Some will be nearly impossible to accept or commit to, so don't. Verify *everything* from your own experience. Do not take our word for anything! You must promise this.

At the same time, keep in mind that you've probably come to this guidebook because you've had enough of what *you've* been doing for however long you've been doing it. You're willing to admit that it hasn't worked, or at least that you're not satisfied with the results. Right?

Keep doing exactly what you are doing or not doing and your future is entirely predictable. Use our book and something else is entirely possible. There is a magic clue on each page.

Just kidding.

There is nothing magical in or about this book, except that right now, at least, you are determined to tell the truth about your own stuckness – your longing for self-love, self-appreciation – and about how sad and frustrated you are with the self-hatred that undermines you at every turn, that inner dialogue that keeps affirming *never good enough*. The fact that you are initially curious about what we may share on the pages ahead is all that is needed for magic to happen.

Shinay and I are obviously still in process, as you are. The women we quote are still in process, and the stories we tell are about process. Maybe we don't undermine ourselves the way we did when we started, but we still find that self-hating thoughts and feelings sneak in between the cracks. We are learning to catch them faster, though, before they have time to implant. We have found that if we are busy loving life, feeding our heart's truest desires, and encouraging and celebrating our longing – the ache of existence – we don't have as much time for self-hatred. These thoughts aren't enemies the way they used to be.

"Take a friendly attitude toward your thoughts," said the Tibetan Buddhist master Chögyam Trungpa Rinpoche. Take a gentle and relaxed attitude toward your self-hatred, we say.

An ideal way to start.

Setting Intention

Take a moment to write down (in your own journal, or on your computer) why you want or need this book, this program. Reflect for a moment about whether or not you are sufficiently tired of being self-hating, and declare for yourself that you are willing to make a Radical Move beyond that.

Shinay Writes

I'm addicted to perfection. I still entertain the notion that once I'm perfect, others will like me...more; I will be worthy of love; I will be beautiful, whole, happy and, best of all, I'll know "who I am." These are all lies, of course. Such a set of equations is absurd. Absolutely! And I know that feeding these lies in an untamed mind leads demons into the heart.

I need this book/this work because I still allow myself to be victimized by these lies. I am writing to remind myself and others of the *real* truth. I've had it up to my eyeballs with my story of *never good enough*.

I declare that it is my job, my birthright, to gather around me the women who will remind me of Woman, of my pristine goodness, and support me in letting go of the lies. Women who will continually encourage me to embrace the *true* story: I am worthy of love, which is my own true nature. I am beautiful in my own unique way. I am good enough just as I am.

RADICAL 1 MOVE

Burn Your Fashion Magazines

When I (Regina) suggested "burn your fashion magazines" as the first Radical Move in this process, Shinay broke into spontaneous applause. Whenever I've mentioned this move in circles of other women, the response has been the same. Together, we all laugh at the obvious implications. Such laughter is healing, if somewhat embarrassing, as we each recognize the extended degree of outward-approval-seeking we do, and the ways in which we waste precious life energy browsing in places where only comparison, false hopes, and dissatisfaction abound.

Fashion mags *per se* aren't really the issue. (Personally, Shinay and I love *Vogue* style, but some of our friends wouldn't know *haute couture* from *haute cuisine*.) With this Move, we are pointing at so much more than the clothes we wear, or the shapeliness of our bodies, or the latest advice on how to be a star in bed. Still, fashion magazines, TV ads, Internet blogs, Facebook, the obsession with the trappings of celebrity culture – all represent a powerful voice, a mindset, of striving to be different while still fitting in; of searching for more, yet feeling that we are *never enough* and therefore looking for approval from others. This voice seems to be hardwired into the cultural mind, and it's broadcast everywhere. We generally grow up in it.

Not only are *we* infected by it, but we pass this infection of "not enough" and "fitting in" along to our daughters and sons, our nieces and nephews, our young friends. We pass it along in the stuff we buy for them, in the expectations we make for them, and primarily in the way we speak about ourselves and about life in general in their presence. They (we) learn it all – the addictions, the worries, the comparisons and judgments, and the endless mirror-gazing for assurance that we're still here and lookin' good.

Even if we were perfect parents, or ultimate mentors, our kids would get bombarded with these voices and mindsets just by walking down the street, watching TV, browsing the Web, going to school. The rain of self-doubt, mistrust, and self-diminishment is falling all around us, and on them. Unless we stop, take our bearings, see where our defenses are weakened... well, it's only a matter of time before we all forget the genuine ache for WOMAN, for our heart's desire, in favor of the quick fix.

We all know, or see, those who have apparently forgotten to check their inner compass, remaining fixated on the standards that others point to. This first Radical Move is about coming home – to ourselves – and dropping for a while those external maps: the images and directions that can both confuse and agitate us. Imagine what it might be like to navigate a trip with a GPS programmed by some perverse alien. (Not a bad plot for a sci-fi drama!) That's a close analogy to what life is like when we lose touch with Woman.

This Radical Move is about intentionally moving away from the bombardment of social standards and taking a new look at our own unique beauty. But even more than challenging the culture's focus on physical appearance, this Radical Move is about clearing out the clutter of our own inner sanctuary and making space for radiance. It's time to throw such phony values in the fire, giving room to the heart's true calling. It's time to turn our attention to something far more worthy of our reverential gaze.

How Pervasive Is It?

We have to see the pothole in the road in order to steer around it. If we insist on driving blind, we'd better be prepared for some heavy shocks. Same with the voices and mindsets of self-hatred. We have to see or hear them as clearly, objectively, and sanely as possible if we want to chart an intentional life course. Otherwise, we're left driving blind, wondering why the bumps are so intense, wondering why we can't seem to get to where we say we want to go.

As you start looking at and listening for the fashion-mag mentality, the *not enoughness*, in whatever form your self-denial comes…and as you begin tracking down its sources over days or weeks, you will be engaging a task that requires courage, along with persistence. This *looking for* and *listening to* is your first assignment in accomplishing this first Radical Move.

Open up a few fashion magazines, read a romance novel, just for the fun of it. Watch TV, go to the movies, surf the Net, spend three or four hours on Facebook, listen to your own conversations, browse the Mall. Look for how *you* are assigning meaning ("*That* might make me happier, slimmer, smarter, sexier… "; "If only…") to what you hear and see. Notice how you feel after engaging these activities. Keep notes for yourself and talk to a woman-friend about what you are seeing, feeling, learning.

For me (Regina), to look at fashion mags as an expression of contemporary art is one thing. I clearly sense whether such browsing nourishes my self-appreciation or not – and sometimes it depends on the day. Do *you* feel inspired, humored, uplifted, expanded in your urgency for life, honoring of yourself and others around you after spending time with this magazine, this person, this environment, or this media source? Or are you left feeling discouraged, dissatisfied, agitated, and even more distressed by self-hatred? What do you learn from doing this? Tell the truth. You really can't expect somebody else to tell you what will feed your self-appreciation, your love, or starve it. Only you can do this.

SOCIAL MEDIA AND DISSATISFACTION

I (Shinay) am what people call a "Millennial" – someone born in the 1980s to early 2000s, who grew up living with digital technology. I'm not a professional researcher, but I have spent hundreds of hours on the Internet for both work and play. I was a late bloomer in this domain – I got my first cellphone when I was nineteen, after I locked myself out of the place where I was housesitting, and had to call for assistance at 1 AM from a payphone at a sketchy gas station.

I have firsthand experience with the boon of social media, particularly in staying connected with others when I travel all over the world. I'm also quite familiar with the downfall of comparing my life with the rose-tinted sliver of a stranger's (and even a friend's) life as revealed on social media. There are times when I judge myself harshly based on the "glossy" images I see on the web. It's a slippery slope for me when it comes to comparing my real life with that of lives portrayed on a communication platform such as Facebook.

With a little help from professional researcher Brené Brown, other authors, and the thousands of articles on the web covering social media and dissatisfaction, I found a few things that are extremely telling about us as a culture in 2016.

From Dr. Brené Brown, Ph.D., author of *Daring Greatly*:

"It's about teaching people that this is not real. We have a basket in our house, a cute wicker basket, and on the top there's a card that says, *Be with the people here, they're amazing.* We collect cellphones because when someone has their phone out, it's basically saying to the other person, you're not the important thing here. Our relationship? Not important. Our time together? Not important. This conversation? Not important. What people don't understand is that we use social media for connection because we're hard wired for connection. But social media is not connection, it's communication. And confusing the two can lead to giving your mobile phone too much emotional power.

So next time a model's sun-kissed bikini Insta-selfie ruins your day, remember, it's her edited life, it's not real. And don't ever compare yourself to strangers on the internet."
(http://www.redonline.co.uk/health-self/self/brene-brown-how-to-beat-instagram-envy).

"...It's challenging to be real in a world that wants us to fit in and please everybody. Authenticity is not a default behavior: It can seem easier just to be what others want us to be, whether that means nodding in agreement when our boss says something we don't actually believe or choosing ridiculously uncomfortable shoes to impress a new group of friends (guilty!)."
(http://www.huffingtonpost.com/2014/09/15/brene-brown-how-to-be-yourself_n_5786554.html)

From Jill DiDonato, author of *Beautiful Garbage:*

> "We live in a culture where at every turn – from our religious beliefs to our peers' admonishments – judgment is *de rigueur.*" (http://www.huffingtonpost.com/jill-di-donato/the-shame-spiral_b_5167300.html)

From Jamie McKillop, *How To Take Control Of Your Digital Life (And Your Real Life)*:

> "Remaining mindful around technology will ultimately lead to higher personal satisfaction." (http://www.huffingtonpost.com/wellgood/how-to-take-control-of-yo_b_9742282.html)

The theme here is mindfulness. I found a great company dedicated to bringing awareness to the divide between "real life" and life portrayed on social media. I like to refer to this choice for awareness as *living beyond social media and enjoying life more.* The company is called *Folk Rebellion,* a lifestyle brand and movement of "Crusading for a return of offline living." Check them out at www.folkrebellion.com.

Part of challenging the lie of *never good enough* is to release what no longer serves us. Judgment, criticism and comparison do not serve our self-respect! Let's start to notice what's not serving us…and let it burn.

ATTENTION IS ALL

Shinay and I have both studied with a brilliant mentor named Red Hawk, a poet and author of fiery books on the subject of self-knowledge. Following his guidance we are both continually reminded of what a precious commodity *human attention* is, and what a precious choice we have in *where and how to place it*. We are learning from Red Hawk that the difference between mediocrity and greatness lies in where and how and with what consistency *we direct our attention*. We have come to appreciate that the placement of attention is a determining factor in whether we realize our life aim, or whether we simply drift; and for us drifting is not the happy alternative. We have done enough of it, flitting from one distraction, one hobby, one spiritual practice to another, or simply channel-surfing or Net-surfing through life.

If you think this practice of looking to see how attention is placed is an easy beginning, however, you are wrong. This self-observation is the most critical orientation of all, and honest explorers in this field of work-on-self will admit that they are still working it, day in and day out. Like that first step in the AA 12-Step programs, unless you are willing to admit that your life (or some aspect of it) has become unworkable, you aren't inclined to start down the path that can ultimately heal you.

For us, admitting that our attention was wasted, misdirected, seduced, forgotten, and manipulated was a bit like calling ourselves indulgent and selfish teenagers. Sounds harsh. The language isn't the best. But the *feeling tone* of what we had to face – the pain of being so unconscious, so ignorant, naïve and lost – is what we wanted to get to. We determined that the worthy placement of our precious human attention was the distinguishing characteristic between an adult woman (Woman) who shone with the light of her own inner being and a grasping immature girl who clung in desperation to the approval of anyone or anything that crossed her path.

Shinay and I are together for a purpose. We have an aim. We invite you to articulate your aim, for yourself and with others. We invite you to notice where *your* attention goes, what robs it, what nurtures it. We know that when our attention is placed on certain *ideas* (like "having it all," like being perfect *whatevers*, like being completely free of care), or on certain *things* (like fashion magazines, or meetings that don't accomplish something, or keeping up with social media), we are robbed of energy and left feeling more hopeless and dissatisfied. We admit to one another, and to our other sisters, that when our attention is "stolen" by some cultural demand, somebody else's standard of success, or some media-driven mindset, we feel powerless, and confirmed in the belief that *we are not enough just as we are.*

On the other hand, when our attention is directed at someone or something that feeds us – in the sense of encouraging us to feel aligned, at home, both strengthened *and* contented, or challenged *and* nurtured – we are happy and powerful. This has become our mutual quest.

WHAT FEEDS SELF-APPRECIATION: A SELF EXAMINATION

Here are some areas to look at as you learn about your own patterns of self-nourishment or deprivation. We beg that you don't try to "fix" what you see or find. The observation alone, with honest evaluation, not negative judgment, is the all-important Radical Move here. Use these as topics of conversation with a trusted friend, or write about them in a journal.

- *Notice your internal dialogues*, those conversations that go on in your head all the time. Particularly notice the dialogues that strengthen self-disregard, as I (Regina) did recently. I was cleaning the house on a Saturday morning when I noticed that I kept up a running dialogue about what a waste of time it was to clean when what I really should be doing was working on this essay for the book.

- *Listen to your own phone calls.* Note to whom, the length, and how you feel at the end of the conversation.
- *Observe your Internet usage,* whether it's e-mail alone, or browsing, Facebook, shopping. Simply find out what happens to your happiness, sense of wholeness, and energy quotient as a result.

From Shinay's Journal

I still get self-conscious when I look at a picture of a beautiful woman. I start to doubt my own radiance and then I start to judge her, negatively, finding fault with her for the fact of her beauty. (*Oh, she's so vain, so full of herself.*)

This downsizing of other women is no way to live.

What gives me the right to sneer and jeer and judge those "other" women on the street, at the table next to mine at the restaurant, or even in the pages of the magazine? How dare I? Where's the solidarity with sister, daughter, mother, auntie, grandma, child; with women of all ages? Where's the compassion?

I see this, I stop.

We are each born of this earth; we will each return to the earth. We are each a unique facet of life expressing Itself, perhaps only for a moment. What's the use in comparison? I tend to belittle what triggers insecurity in me, or what I am jealous of. It's a bad habit but it gives me a false sense of elevation and worthiness. I see this, I stop.

I have been "that woman" on the receiving end of others' negativity, gossip, and jealousy. I feel sad for WOMAN who must endure this.

I see this, I stop.

- *Monitor your reading,* magazine skimming, even browsing in bookstores or libraries. Some of us are never satisfied until we make ourselves crazy with how much there is to read, and how little time we have to do it. Does reading feed you (which types) or exhaust you (which types)?

- *Note your view of other women,* including the shape and strength of their bodies, their intelligence, their accomplishments. Basically, this is about noting the way in which you are making comparisons and finding yourself either better or worse than others. How does that leave you feeling? This might be as much about their apparently advanced spiritual status as about their fashion expertise, so look for all of it. Just observe. Learn about yourself!

- *Witness your shopping* for clothes, shoes, or accessories; your beauty-enhancement rituals, your hair time, nail time. How much time in the course of a week, of a month, is spent in beautifying, and how much in fantasizing about beautifying? Talk this one over, or write about it, and keep laughing. No "bad" judgments, just honest assessment of what nurtures you and what drains you.

SIMPLE, NOT EASY

It is radical to really see and tell the truth about how our attention is scattered and how skewed our vision and appreciation of ourselves has become. Mediocrity within yourself and its external media-messengers will fight hard to keep you following the herd. The lies we continue to tell ourselves, and the negative stories we reinforce by the images of happiness we surround ourselves with, are pervasive and insidious. When instead we choose to see *what is* about ourselves – seeing the frequency with which we abandon the source, the center – we place ourselves within a small circle of radical pathfinders. When we see how big this No of "not enough" is, and admit how it is robbing us of ourselves, we've already stepped away from it. With awareness comes movement. Naturally, once you see the pothole you steer around it!

Open your eyes to what's out there in the environment – what's screaming at you, what's demanding your money, what's stealing your precious attention away from the wondrous things you say you most treasure. As Shinay and I have learned, you won't be able to step over self-depreciation until you're willing to see clearly how you're getting used by the voices or parasitic mindsets that bombard you. This is serious business. Take courage. And…

LIGHTEN UP

Relaxation, gentleness and a sense of humor are essential here, which is why we make a silly suggestion (like burning fashion magazines) right from the start. The more you see about your lost attention and your patterns of comparison and self-hatred, the more you may be inclined to tense up, become judgmental, give in to seriousness about what you are discovering. That's why "Lighten up" is a really important mantra for this first Radical Move. Use it. Remind your friends and sisters to use it. It's normal that you will try to apply your old hardball strategies to this new softball game. Give 'em up! These old moves of trying harder, making more demands on yourself, and self-blame haven't worked too well, so share a laugh about them if you can.

On the other hand, the recognition of these old strategies can turn them into our allies. As we notice them, they alert us to the need for honesty and relaxation. Being uncomfortable, finding ourselves mucking around in the old swamp, is a vital part of this engagement with radical life. As one wise woman told us: "Until we see how lost we are we won't turn around and look for another road."

Never Good Enough

At our coffeehouse meeting in November, I (Regina) was discouraged. The writing wasn't happening, as I'd just spent weeks focusing on another project. Also, I had just seen several TED talks by fantastic speakers who tackled this issue of self-hatred with sterling clarity. I was no longer confident that I had anything of value to offer. I had fallen into "not good enough."

When I sat down with Shinay and started to tell her how I felt, she grinned with excitement. Then she demanded that I write her a letter, on the spot, listing all of my inadequacies. I opened my notebook and started my diatribe of complaint, comparison and fear. At the same time, she began a letter to me, writing furiously fast. We stopped after ten minutes and read our pieces to one another.

As I read mine, she smiled even more broadly; apparently, what she had written was an exact counterpoint to my whining. As she read hers, I was not only inspired, but laughing. She was unwilling to accept my small vision of myself and my protest of inadequacy as a writer, or my opinions about myself as a hypocrite or fraud rather than as an elder with some wisdom. She was adamant that our book was needed, maybe not as an internationally acclaimed podcast, but by the women in her yoga classes, her friends and our peers around the world.

Before my tea had cooled, the whole world looked different. Our honest sharing had re-inspired my courage to move ahead.

A RITUAL BURNING

There is no transformation without heat and pressure. The Sanskrit word *tapas* means "to burn." In the context of yoga practice, Shinay reminds her students that we talk about *tapas* as burning away the impurities in the body, mind, and emotions. There is great discipline and tenacity required, yet there is also tremendous passion. It is the heat of passion that brings us the fire of love. This is the fieriness that gets our hearts pumping and heightens our desire to move beyond the *blah, blah, blah*, paving the way to our own true nature.

It is one thing to talk metaphorically about the need to "burn" fashion magazines (or other input sources) in order to move beyond the sense of "not enough." But, to actually give something up, or to set something on fire, is quite another level of radical!

Ritual, however, is part of all our lives – whether it is the ritual of a birthday celebration or the ritual of a hot bath. And fire is one of the most powerful agents of change in the world, which is why it is incorporated into religious rituals from nearly all spiritual traditions. As we exercise to transform our bodies, in fact, we even talk about "feeling the burn."

Shinay and I recommend that you join us in creating some tangible form to express your commitment to loving yourself. Make the radical move to burn something – anything – that symbolizes the old *blah blah blah* and notifies both yourself and the powers that be (the Universe, the goddess, the angels, whomever you love and trust, or some higher power) that you are intent on moving beyond comparison and self-loathing.

In the spiritual tradition in which we two are based, the use of certain fire rituals is both practical and celebratory. We participate in a *yajna* or purification fire ceremony about once a year. Together with friends and family (children love this part), we gather the old stuff of the past and offer it to the flames. Some of us might burn the love letters from a relationship gone sour; others burn photos, notebooks, unopened packs of cigarettes, an item of clothing that contains unhealthy attachments. Still others write up lists of the things they would like to clear up: messy relationships, addictions, unexpressed grief. I remember one such fire where a good friend burned a perfectly good pair of leather boots, much to my horror. Though she never shared why, over time I came to honor her choice to make such a radical break with some aspect of her past.

Burning things up may not be your thing. But you could ritualize your break with old programming by digging a hole and burying something that represents it. You could take your

Burning Issues

The first time I (Shinay) did a ritual burning was when I completed high school. I was nineteen years old. It was graduation night and I sat in my backyard with my friend Sera. Just the two of us. I didn't want to go to any of the big parties, I didn't want to go out and celebrate. I wanted to clear out the clutter and make room for whatever newness lay ahead. I took my graduation cap and gown, my yearbooks, my old notebooks, even old photographs, all the cute-boy clippings, and art projects I had done, and they all went into the fire. Sera and I sat in silence for a very long time. She knew what I was up to. We held each other and watched the stuff burn. After all, it was just stuff. The next day I felt free, alive, clear and without a hangover like the rest of my peeps. I was beginning something new, without knowing what to expect.

stuff or simply your *blah-blah-blah* song to the ocean or another moving body of water and send it sailing away. You could climb a hill and release it to the wind. You could put on loud music and dance and sweat it off until you stop from exhaustion. Then, take a shower or a bath.

Doing such a ritual alone is one thing. Sharing it with a resonant friend is another. Joyfully, tenderly, you can support one another in solidifying your intention, your aim. Make it an event to remember. Some of us like to use flowers, incense, ritual objects like feathers and crystals, chants or song. Be creative.

Have fun.

DEEPENING THE MOVE

Years ago, I (Regina) heard a wise woman talk about the dead end of comparison, and the suffering it caused. This woman noted that, no matter how beautiful and accomplished we might ever become, it wouldn't take long before another woman showed up in our vicinity who was more so: more beautiful, more accomplished, more "spiritual," more more. This was the nature of life. This example was a commentary on the reality of impermanence: that nothing lasts forever. (Think of some gorgeous movie actress from three decades ago. Get the picture? All things pass.) It was also a reflection on the suffering we inflict upon ourselves by our vise-strong notions about who we are, our full-on attachments to what we currently have, and our grasping for what we think we need. Even those who think they are beautiful and accomplished, or know they are rich, must struggle to stay that way. And forever. Good luck!

Even those who are applauded for being beautiful and accomplished often still feel like a fraud; they too resort to grasping to keep from being found out. For those of us who don't think we are all that beautiful or accomplished, there is grasping for something else – anything – that will compensate. And when the strategies for compensation don't work, there can be depression, along with cynicism toward others and about life in general; and resignation to being "less than" forever. These are the high prices we pay for denying impermanence, and for trying to justify the lie of *never good enough.*

As we conclude this first chapter, we invite you to take the consideration just one step deeper to honestly look at what your current dissatisfaction, your self-hatred, rests on. For example: Is your self-hatred really a statement that you, out of so many fortunate others, were handed a raw deal by luck or God? Or how about: Does your dissatisfaction with yourself imply that you are somehow flawed and therefore unlovable? That you were denied the discipline gene? Intelligence? Grace? Money? Circumstances?

Try to reach underneath this generic blanket of *never good enough* to tickle the mistaken beliefs – more lies – that hide there. Be honest (and gentle and humorous!) with yourself, and perhaps with your trusted friend. Be honest about the fact that you may still be holding these notions as real truths about yourself, not as the lies they are. Just for the "fun" of it, argue to support such a victimized life, and don't give up too easily. Indulge a bit in telling why you actually warrant self-hatred more than others! If you can keep your sense of humor and your perspective, then the trap of comparison with others, the experience of dissatisfaction with what is, and the self-hatred that result can actually become invaluable tools for self-remembrance.

Shinay and I assert that dissatisfaction with ourselves, just like all other forms of self-created suffering, is a result of ego-clinging to an unrealistic view of the world, and of oneself. This clinging lies at the root of our unhappiness. We mistakenly think that we are somehow special distinct entities, separate individuals awaiting our turn in the Miss Universe contest. We mistakenly believe that there *is* such a thing as the most beautiful woman in the world, who stays that way forever; that there is some ideal or some perfectly unruffled life. And, we conclude that we could (or should?) be this, or have this, if only we knew the right formula...or had the right stuff, like knowledge, good hair, straight teeth, plenty of money (or whatever brand of stuff we sense is lacking).

Take the time to enumerate the lies you've latched onto and to explore the beliefs they mistakenly rest on. Then, burn something to signify your intention to move forward.

RADICAL CONTENTMENT

There is a Bible psalm (number 131, to be exact) about resting in the arms of Love; about being happy to be exactly where we are, not concerning ourselves with "great" things that are currently above our payscale. Let's call it "the song of radical contentment," which is the art and practice of being with what is, and being grateful for it. Radical contentment is not an excuse to hold ourselves as less, or small, or a ploy for playing it safe, without risk. Actually, such a deep commitment to contentment is probably far riskier than bungee jumping or starting a new business venture. Actions that arise from radical contentment are often actions with a longer-term possibility. They have a genuine foundation on which miracles can build.

Great things are not necessarily media-worthy. In fact, many great lives were characterized by small simple activity, gentle attention, compassion in speech to all. Like a certain Japanese monk (Sodo Yokoyama) who lived in the latter part of the twentieth century. He spent his adult life sitting under a tree in a Kyoto park, meditating and playing sweet music with a leaf flute (he placed two leaves together and blew air through them to create a haunting sound). Sodo Yokoyama attracted the attention of children at play and was often surrounded by a circle of them. He spread happiness and beauty from his solitary spot, and was honored and even loved by all who encountered him.

> *All you have to do is decide that wherever you are is the best place there is. Once you start comparing one place to another, there's no end to it.*
>
> – Sodo Yokoyama

A Story of Radical Contentment

I (Shinay) was twenty-three when I chose to go back to school. Prescott College, a small private liberal arts college in my hometown, where my mom, dad, sister and her family still resided, was the perfect choice. I'd already traveled around the world a few times and wanted to be closer to home.

One of the great things about Prescott College is that each new student participates in a wilderness orientation instead of sitting in a classroom for the first month. So, in January of 2010, I found myself in a group of nine (including instructors) on a three-week backpacking trip into the Grand Canyon National Park and the Superstition Mountains south of Tucson.

During the course of those three weeks we talked about the "Solo" – a three-day experience each new student would have. Our instructors chose a secluded area of wilderness for each of us, away from eyesight yet within earshot of one another. Separate, yet together.

Each area was clearly defined by natural landmarks or by cairns so that we would not wander off. The point was internal retreat, not "get lost in the wilderness." The only items we were allowed to take with us were our sleeping bag, sleeping mat, a tarp, one piece of light reading material (we were backpacking, after all), a journal and toilet paper. We also had the option to make our own meals or to fast during this time.

I chose to fast. I wanted the full experience. For seventy-two hours I laid around, most of the time naked, with my journal, writing and watching the sky. It was an experience I'd never had before. I was free to be me and it didn't matter *who* I chose to be. The wilderness didn't care about my scars or the shape of my butt or the fact that all I thought about was food.

As the hours passed, I was soon overwhelmed with gratitude for being alive; flooded with a sense of power, as if the molten core of the Earth had somehow gotten into my bloodstream. I was alive. I was not afraid. I was filled with self-love.

When I finally rejoined the group, I was ecstatic. I felt that if I died at that very moment I would want for nothing. I was elated and filled with a deep sense of fullness and gratitude for those who walked this path before me. Those seventy-two hours I will treasure for the rest of my life. I was belly-down in the dirt with nothing on but my heartbeat. . .and I was content.

When we "burn" our fashion magazines, we signal to the Universe that we are ready for a different kind of conversation, one that is beyond comparison. Any time you need a reminder to do that, let this book be there for you. Call on us, and/or find a friend, which is the subject of our next Radical Move. Transformation lasts when we surround ourselves with similarly intentioned, real-life women. With Woman. Ditch the glossy pages and go find some other fleshy bodies to hang around. It's good for your soul.

Find an Interrupting Friend

I (Regina) need a friend. Especially at times when I get lost in the labyrinth of my own confused mind. A few months ago, a terse e-mail from an associate threw me off, and seriously. I couldn't seem to get back on the track of self-esteem and began to spiral down into entertaining the lie of *not good enough*. My associate had apparently misunderstood what I considered to be my best intentions and misinterpreted in the worst possible way the actions I had felt to be genuinely compassionate. I was sad. But angry, too. I blamed him. *Why does he...? Why doesn't he...?* And the conclusion I came to was that, because I wasn't appreciated and was probably causing more harm than good, I should therefore quit my role in the project that he and I were working on together. That would show him! On and on my mind raved with conclusions, interpretations and ultimatums, until the knot in my solar plexus was solid. I felt sick. I didn't want to work. I was temporarily paralyzed. If he didn't appreciate me, probably nobody did. My life was worthless.

I called Nancy. A few years older than me, a few more turns in the spiral of life, yet she actually considers me a mentor, and I consider her the same. We're good together. Nancy, too, suffers periodically in getting bogged down in these insane *samskaras* (the Sanskrit word for "mind tracks"). Like me, she knows better. But she also doesn't expect that life is ever going to be a smooth sail. Doldrums happen, as do thunderstorms. Mind at peace. Mind in turmoil. So it goes.

Nancy is also a committed listener. She will not turn away, no matter how crazy I sound. More wonderful still, she will not try to make me feel better; not try to assuage me by saying how much she loves me; not try to build my case about how inconsiderate and mean this associate has been to me. She won't tell me that I have lots of other friends, and therefore shouldn't take his word as something to get upset about. She won't tell me this is all foolishness and I should just be strong.

What she does is simply affirm that she too knows this pattern of mind, this path of insanity. What she does is invite me to leave the mind's stories and move into the feelings, the sensations, the contractions in the body, the way in which the breath is currently rising and falling, and to stay with that focus as much as I can. She reminds me of a powerful teaching from one of our mutual and highly respected teachers, Arnaud Desjardins. *Be one with the emotion.* Don't try to work it out through the mind. There is no healing at the level of mind. Stay with the body.

Her counsel is wise. She hasn't tried to fix the content of my problem. Instead she's addressed the context for liberating myself from such deadly meanderings. She has interrupted my mind stream. She's called me home to practice in the way that we've agreed will ultimately serve one another. I treasure this interruption, a self-imposed interruption. Such interruptions are essential, the gift of fellow pilgrims on the path.

A month from now, when Nancy is needing wise counsel, I'll be there for her in the same way. In between, we each have to do our own work with these tendencies. We each have to deal with the invitations to self-loathing that fill our inboxes and our minds. And, we celebrate the role of ally we play for one another. This is hard work.

Three Months Later

Just as I (Regina) was opening my computer for a day's work I got a phone call from Nancy. Her voice was weak. "Do you have a moment?" she inquired, apologetically. When I tell her that I'm all here for her, I can hear her taking a deep breath. Then, as she speaks, this glorious and powerful friend is all timid and hesitating. "I'm really needing to talk to you," she says. "I'm in a pit of discouragement, feeling like I've lost my work."

This "lost my work" thing is a biggie for both of us. "Work" is spiritual work, or spiritual practice. For years we heard this clarion call to "protect your work" from our own much-loved spiritual teacher. It was a call meant to rouse us from lethargy, to remember the essence of our path, to keep us focused on paying attention! But because we have old ears that hear blame and shame in any kind of demand, because we operate from never enough, we easily fell – still fall – into using this battle cry as a way to find ourselves bad and wrong. Nancy was in it. Fortunately, on that day, I was not.

"Oh, fantastic!" I said, much to her surprise. The silence that blossomed on the other end of the phone was deafening, so I went on. "You're right on schedule! I could have predicted this."

"What are you talking about?" Nancy was starting to sound a little defensive.

I explained.

In the past few months I'd begun to consider the subject of merely aging versus growing in wisdom. My study and my own experience had verified that "second half of life" spirituality had marked stages. Nancy, as an elder, was right in the middle of it.

"You are being dis-illusioned," I ventured. She listened. "We all have to lose even our high-minded notions of God in order for the real God to live in us. Whatever 'work' you thought you had as a younger woman is being challenged at the deepest level. This is exactly what is supposed to happen. I join you in this."

Nancy was weeping on the other end of the phone line by the time I finished. She never expected such a response. I didn't realize I knew all this until she asked for help. Amazing grace spoke through me, apparently.

Suffice it to say that I was happy to reciprocate the favor of friendship that Nancy had offered to me only three months earlier. I had interrupted her life, her dead-end program of failure and loss, in a way that was serving to both of us.

THE INTERRUPTIONS THAT COUNT

A really true friend is one who will interrupt your life, and forever. Not "interrupt" as in calling you on the phone just as you're putting dinner on the table, or in showing up at your door repeatedly and unannounced. This Radical Move is about finding, or affirming *and being*, the kind of friend who will interrupt the old familiar replay of the "never enough" routine: you agree to interrupt hers, if she will interrupt yours.

Who in your life *now* invites, or even demands, that you put down this "not good enough" script? Who will interrupt you when the *blah blah blah* takes over? Where is the friend who sees you for *who you are* and will call you back to that remembrance? Who are you willing to do this for? Who won't desert you even when you've temporarily deserted yourself? Who will you stand by, forever? Does someone immediately come to mind? Call her up now and tell her how much you appreciate her. Don't wait!

This second Radical Move is about declaring what already is, if indeed you have such a friend, or putting out the call/ holding the intention to locate or create that friend, even if you fear that no such friend exists (which is just another part of the lie of self-sufficiency and independence that the culture reinforces). It is also about being that interrupting friend for another, or others, once the bond is established and affirmed.

For some of us, this Radical Move will require little effort, except perhaps to articulate our promises to one another. (*Have you called her yet?*) We may want to establish a few dates to be together – in person or on the phone – to affirm our commitments to interruption, and perhaps to work on some of these Radical Moves together.

For others, the idea of reaching out to ask for any kind of help, to acknowledge that we may need such a friend, to risk creating or deepening such a bond, may be the most disagreeable task imaginable. Please relax. Lighten up. No pressure here. Just read on and consider a few possibilities.

Going It Alone

Are we all in agreement here that attempting a climb to the top of Mt. Everest alone amounts to sheer idiocy? Sure, there have been individuals who made the solitary ascent, and some even without supplemental oxygen. *And*, let's be honest, some of the best of them became disoriented from altitude sickness and made a critical error of judgment that resulted not only in their own death but in the deaths of those who attempted to rescue them.

The telling factor here, on Mt. Everest and in any serious attempt at conquest of any kind, is that unconscious influences (like the need to prove something to a domineering father) kick in when the air gets thin and the thinking-mind muddled. At 20,000 feet, after a number of hours alone in sub-freezing conditions, the climber who has dropped one of her gloves or her goggles often doesn't even know that she *has* dropped one of her gloves or her goggles. She simply accommodates and pushes on, or lies down to sleep, or decides to jump off the cliff. She simply doesn't know that she is seriously impaired in all of her faculties. A companion, a guide, another climber who points out the impairment to her may mean the difference between life and death.

The explorer in the domain of self-understanding can also become seriously confused, or deluded. "Following the wrong god home we may miss our star," says the poet William Stafford. And the voice of the heart, that god still and soft within, while itself essentially true, can also be easily distorted or co-opted by unconscious factors. The need to be perfect, or regret for past "sins" are not the least of such unconscious motivations.

Going it alone is another of those unspoken and rarely questioned foundations of our cultural milieu.

Going it alone *should* be understood as a necessity when we realize that nobody else is going to do the work of self-acceptance for us. On the other hand – the all-too-common hand – the banner of "going it alone" is more frequently waved by those who are simply, often profoundly, afraid – afraid of being rejected, again; afraid of being seen as weak; afraid of being misunderstood and hurt in any way. Ultimately, afraid of being interrupted in a way that will require risk, a stretch outside a familiar comfort zone. Relationships are messy. Other women might not understand what you're talking about or asking for. You might get close and then lose somebody to a move or to death, or *blah blah blah*. It *is* a big risk!

Stronger Together

When Regina first asked me to co-author this book with her, I (Shinay) was shocked and honored. Shocked: Who was I, so inexperienced, so naïve to write about self-hatred? Honored: Regina saw something in me, and her request was not to be taken lightly. We needed each other, she and I, because Regina had come to a standstill and I needed to be stretched: to grow up and put my big-girl panties on. It's almost as if the Universe preferred that this book be a joint effort and demanded that we not try to go at it alone. Those voices asking, "What do I have to offer the world that's worth anything?" are loud and persistent in each of us. Together, however, we are stronger than the voices. We remind one another of our intrinsic greatness, our worthiness. Alone, I fall victim to the lie more easily; after all, it's only my own voice I have to listen to. It takes great courage to step out of the hell I've created for myself. It takes great strength to tell myself a new story of worthiness. Regina reminds me of the choice I have to make every day. Every moment of every day. Each time the voice of self-loathing creeps in, I have a decision to make: the decision to hate myself or to live beyond my own self-limiting patterns. I need this book as much as any of our readers do. We wrote this for ourselves. We write this for each other.

Assuming a position of radical independence, feeling like you need to prove something, or enforced isolation are also really risky. I (Regina) am learning this clearly as I age. I'm not so good any more at driving alone late at night. I live out in the desert of northern Arizona, at the edge of the grid, with no highway lights or street lamps. Long stretches of two-lane road where the speed limit is 70 mph must be navigated. At midnight, heading back home from a gathering of friends, I will play loud music or listen to talk-radio and struggle to stay awake. Still, I've scared myself once or twice with a minute swerve that sent me onto the shoulder. There is no margin for error out there. I need to admit that this activity isn't serving my highest intentions and get a friend to travel with me.

Throughout this book, Shinay and I plead the case for listening within, and for eschewing that external standard that has us all jumping through hoops. Without diminishing these pleas in the slightest, we beg you to consider or reconsider the value of the wise friend, the caring witness, the guide or teacher on the path. After all, even the greatest ones among us – from Mother Teresa and Nelson Mandela to other brilliant humanitarians, artists, saints, even buddhas – have had one or more companions or teachers who guided them in their search. The desert fathers and desert mothers of the early Christian hermetical tradition practiced devotion, surrender, and obedience to an elder. Even in the rare instances when the younger monk's realization was more advanced than the mentor's, he or she embraced surrender and obedience to the spiritual mother or spiritual father as much as possible because the bond in itself was a reflection of humility and grace.

The poet Rumi said that "there are a thousand ways to kneel and kiss the ground." In other words, there are a thousand ways to love and serve and celebrate. Left to our own devices,

A Soul Sister

Libby is my better half. I (Shinay) say this with affection because we complement each other so well. We once tried to date the same guy without even knowing it! (We only found out later.) Libby is a soul sister, connected at the heart.

Every time I see Libby in person (about once every three years) she greets me with a wiggle and a giggle. I treasure the joy Libby exudes as she dances toward me, all lightness in being. To meet and greet her in the same spirit in which she approaches me is a practice in overcoming self-hatred.

Self-depreciation is *so serious*, Libby reminds me. "The trick is to shake your booty...shake your shoulders, give your legs a little dance and wiggle." We dance. Her playfulness is an easy way to get beyond the *blah, blah, blah* and back to my essential nature – my *groove thang*. I recommend it to you, too, no matter how old you are. Try doing a little dance, a little wiggle, the next time you see "your" girls.

When Libby and I talk over the phone our conversation is mostly giggling. Our laughing is not *blah-blah*. It is breakthough! I don't need to pretend to be other than who I am with her. When our laugher quiets, Libby says things like, "Don't worry, it will all work out," and "Be true to yourself," and "Find the answer in your heart." The way she says it is real. She reminds me of what I already know and brings me back to my body and my breath and the whole complete goddess I already am. I just need a little reminder.

most of us would easily come up with a dozen or more ways to love – to honor creation – in our lifetime. Maybe even fifty! But a thousand? *A thousand ways* means that life as we know it has been exploded, in the best way possible. *A thousand ways* means that self-doubt and "never enough" are overwhelmed by the knowledge that *everything* is sacred.

Like the companion on the mountain, the authentic friend can point out the danger signals that our enthusiasm (or pride) is causing us to overlook. They can help us carry a heavy pack. They can help us clear away a spot to rest for the night, warn us about proximity to cliff edges, and call us to attention when we've neglected to put on our goggles against snow blindness. Along the trail, she can also point out the gorgeous scenery, dance with us when the music plays, and invite us to undertake various projects that we might never have imagined we could do.

A true friend is a constant *Yes* to the force of love in the world, as we can be that for her. We remind one another that we are not separate from the One, the Love, even while we may argue with one another and fight to defend our limitations.

If you do *not* have such a friend, or feel that you are not that friend for another, sharpen your intention, wait patiently, read, and talk to someone whose judgment and clarity you trust about this issue. Pray for guidance to what the future may hold for you. Try to never say "never" about anything. If you *do* want such a friend, but haven't found *the* one, make a cry to heaven for this intention. Pray.

There is so much joy in having companions in doing this work. Certainly there are risks; there are untrustworthy individuals. But you're bright. Wake up. Abuse is not acceptable, but a challenge to ego should be a painful sting, and that's what you come to the genuine friend for. Don't stay in the foothills when you can ascend the slopes.

Rabia's Story

Shinay's mom, Rabia, recently came back from a week in Washington D.C. visiting her four sisters and told Shinay this story:

The four of us were sitting on the couch in Carol's living room on Saturday afternoon. We were all barefoot, with wine glasses in hand, and bemoaning one of our key genetic traits – curved big toes. Our gossip mode was full on. Arlene started in about her weight, Mary Ellen chimed in with, "Well my feet..." and Susan added, "My back... ." It was a negative self-talk *fiesta!* and I'd had enough. I, the eldest, decided to halt that conversation before it went off the cliff.

Normally, I would have added my fair share of *blah, blah, blah* to show them that I was in just as bad shape as they (if not worse off), but my self-love angel was there that day and I abruptly got up from the couch and playfully yet sincerely said to them, "I'm not going down that road. If we're going to continue the complaining, I'm out. No more blah, blah, blah."

Shocked and relieved, my sisters went silent. Then we all burst out laughing and moved on to talking about our children. I would have preferred we went a little deeper into the wants and desires of mothers with grown children, but at least it was a start. If we couldn't speak kindly about ourselves, we wouldn't say anything at all. Maybe next time I'll start a conversation about how much I love my hands because...

Shinay writes: My mother is one of those women you want to have around when the conversation has gone stale because she knows the value in forging friendships that keep us afloat instead of sinking with our own self-hatred ship.

SHAME ISOLATES

For many of us, the self-hatred we are considering here comes from deeply rooted shame. We can't "make it" in the way that others seem to make it, and we are therefore ashamed. We can't seem to keep up, as others seem able to, with our exercise programs, our diets, our resolutions to be kinder to our children, our three jobs. We can't forget the many ways in which we've hurt ourselves, or others, and the many disappointments we've caused, to ourselves and others, over years. The not-good-enough-mother idea is an ongoing example of this. This shame is doubly toxic because we think we might be better off by hiding it and putting on a strong front. Our shame will either isolate us to keep from exposing itself, or we will try harder and harder to keep up appearances to avoid having to see it, deal with it, step beyond it. As one of my mentors used to say, we're "looking good but going nowhere."

Dr. Brené Brown, whom we mentioned in the previous chapter, author of the book *Daring Greatly*, stunned the modern world with one simple formula given via a TED talk several years ago. Her reflection on the connection between vulnerability and the healing of shame was not new. Alcoholics Anonymous and dozens of other programs, including various sacraments or rituals in many of the world's religions, have made the same or similar distinctions. Brené's message was upbeat, secular, clear – and self-revelatory. She courageously admitted that, despite years of research into the nature of shame, she herself was its victim. In her talk, she became a messenger of the right moment, and her simple and honest words touched millions of people the world over.

What we don't talk about or admit to builds a faulty foundation on which we attempt to construct a meaningful life. Read that again. Thank you. *This doesn't work.* It isolates us from our own deepest love, and from the love of others. It's as if we're wearing a T-shirt that says on the front *Don't Come Any Closer* and on the back *If You Really Knew Me You'd Be Disappointed.* (What does your T-shirt say?)

We don't share our pain or our disappointments because we have confused being vulnerable with being weak. However we came to learn that equation and started basing our life on it doesn't matter. Fact is, we got it. Being weak was not allowed, and that nixed the vulnerability end of the formula. The equation itself was another lie, and a dangerous one. Seriously believed, it has the power to sicken us, or even kill us.

Our friend Cecilia is a classic loner. Her shame at not being good enough shows up in her constant weight-gain/weight-loss cycles. She frankly admits that she hates her body and hates the sense that she is out of control, undisciplined, and stuck. She says she *wants* to look better, to feel better, to reach out and be touched, but shame and comparison – meaning fear of the judgments of others – keeps her in a tiny box, doing the *same 'ole same 'ole,* day after day. It is very lonely in that box.

Certainly it is counterintuitive for someone like Cecilia to join a group when being around other women is exactly what encourages this stress of self-hatred for her. Logically, it appears better to stay in her tiny box, safe and isolated, and suffer her own fate, trying to figure things out for herself. She lives with a high defense quotient. So I ask her, "And how is life in the box working out for you so far?" To which she will admit, at least to me, "It isn't."

Perhaps she is not desperate enough yet. Maybe she has to hit another bottom line before she's ready for an interrupting friend. This crash might not be pretty, though, and as much as I'd like to protect her from more pain, I can't. She is living inside of a lie. It will take great courage to get out, but not as much as she may have imagined. This Radical Move for her will start by making herself vulnerable to another, a caring other who will not try to rescue her but will give her the feedback of silent respect – feedback that her vulnerability is actually the act of a courageous woman, not a weak woman. Unless we admit to being in prison, there's no possibility of applying for parole.

In the meantime, I love her and will hold her in my heart as being a hurting sister, not a weak sister. And when she *is* desperate, or when that "bottom" slams against her, I'll be here for her, as my own circle of support will be here for me.

SAVING OUR FRIENDS

Have you ever seen a dog chasing its own tail? Wiggling in a tight, frenzied circle? It's funny, until it becomes pathetic. The only way to distract the poor creature is to make a loud noise or throw a ball and make the dog stop spinning long enough to start running in another direction. Our minds are the same way. In a state of downwardly spiraling self-talk, or *blah blah* complaint-conversation with our companions, we are no better than dogs chasing their tails or hamsters running on a wheel. We need our real friends (interrupting friends) to pull us out of ourselves, to rescue us from the edge and remind us how to stand on our own two feet.

I (Shinay) used to think I had to bend over backward to please my friends. I would go out of my way to make sure they liked me. I've since learned to surround myself with fabulous bad-asses. I hang out with bright, life-affirming, butt-kicking, brilliant, talented, funny and gorgeous women. We have to know (and learn) when to be disciplined and when to surrender. Friends remind us of our greatness. Friends bring us out of our heads and invite us to live more from a place of connection. This potential lies within each of us, within every relationship

– in some more than others. If you walk away from a tea date or hang-out session feeling more depressed and lonely and drained than you were previously, we suggest you reconsider your relationship agreement – perhaps reconsider the benefit and the contribution you make to each other. Ultimately, the people in our lives are not the ones holding us back from being our radical, vibrant, luminous selves. It's our own choice to stay around them, to please them, to reinforce their self-defeating programs that makes it hard to break free!

It doesn't interest me…

How busy you are and why
Your excuses that justify a lack of integrity
    around time or a lack of communication
Why you forgot
How hard you "tried"
Your complaints about others
Why you failed
The pain you experienced physically from
    an old operation or ordeal
Why you can't control your temper
Why the day is miserable
Your excuse for being insensitive
Why you are right and they are wrong
Why you are late
Why you can't help it
Why you are lazy
Your justifications for being unhealthy
Your "story" about any situation
What you blame your mood on
Why you hate people in general or some specific person

Why you can't let something go
Why you can't keep silent
Why you don't speak up
Your story about being a victim
Your language that keeps things in place
Your unwillingness to listen and receive
The words "never" and "always"
The words "can't" and "won't."

— Lesley Ball

Are your relationships encouraging you to stay in the rut of self-defeat, or are your friends reminding you to move beyond negative self-talk, be more kind to others, and live the life you've always wanted? Choose.

Donna's Friends

All she needed was a willing ear. In fact, she begged us to offer no comments, especially advice. The only feedback she requested was our full attention, without sighs of empathy, with bright presence and appreciation for how she was exploring the issue for herself.

Donna was overwhelmed, she said. She simply wanted two intelligent witnesses to hear about how her life felt out of control. She needed to vent, to rant, to cry, to complain, to try helplessly to reason things out for herself. Most of all, she needed to do this in the presence of caring others who would not judge her as less, or try to fix her. So she asked for it. She went to the trouble of making a date with the two of us, and giving herself a time limit (forty minutes), after which we would simply sit silently and then have tea together.

And so she talked about how difficult it was to be a good mother to an active five-year-old, and how she doubted herself in this venture. She cried about how insecure she felt in dealing with her husband's teenagers who lived with them. She explained to us how hard it was to avoid blaming her partner for the pressures she felt. She moaned that she had little time for her own silence and art.

We just loved her, and said nothing.

She got quiet and wept softly. Then, she opened her eyes, looked at us, and thanked us for the sweet gift of our presence and attention. "I know what I want to do," she said.

Donna had arrived at a first next-step all by herself. She told us about it. We listened some more without comment.

Then we made tea.

A GENERATIVE CONVERSATION

In March of 2013, I (Regina) came up with the acronym WASH (Women Addressing Self-Hatred) as a way to characterize what I had been seeing and feeling in myself and other women for longer than I could remember. As accomplished as we women are, we are our own worst critics. We talk in ways that betray ourselves. We don't speak as if we love ourselves. In fact, many of us speak with an edge of self-hatred.

Shinay and I got a laugh out of the spelling WASH, since women have forever been the ones washing the clothes – our own and those of the whole family. Women have gathered for ages along the riverbanks to pound their clothes clean on the rocks. They have walked long distances, drawing water at the village well, to bathe and nourish their families. In industrialized countries, keeping our children's clothes clean has certainly become an obsession, and a sure sign of being a "good mother."

The word WASH has many implications. Certainly, the idea is inherent that we might "wash" ourselves of the old lingering habits of self-deprecation by gathering with one or more other women to "do the wash."

In the summer of 2014, shortly after determining that we would do this project together, we agreed to start a conversation about the subject of self-hatred by creating a pin bearing the acronym WASH. The intent was never to start a national movement. Neither of us was interested in that. The idea was simply to spark a dialogue with other women...or men – with anyone who might ask us about the meaning of the pin – as a way to gather data in preparation for writing this book together.

WASH is an invitation to a conversation. That's all.

The conversation concerns an individual woman's recognition that self-hatred has its hooks in her. It's an invitation for her to speak about that, in whatever way she wishes.

The conversation is one she can and probably does often have with herself, but the invitation of WASH is to join at the riverbank, or at the village well, and have that conversation with other women; to exchange with those who share the same issue and a desire to be out from under this burden.

A conversation about self-hatred and the commitment to challenge it is not a sharing of mutual advice, although that is bound to happen. Nonetheless, advising is discouraged, because sharing advice starts to quickly set up ranks: the women who have "the good advice" and give it out freely, and the women who think they don't have "the advice" already, and look to someone else to supply it. Some women are so desperate or naïve they will take any foolish advice without passing it through the heart of their own innate wisdom. Some women don't recognize, let alone trust, that they have innate wisdom, of any kind. These are particularly difficult cases.

No. The WASH conversation would ideally focus on the energy drain that self-negation fosters. It would not essentially be about what *put* the notion of self-hatred there in the first place. That is the domain of therapy or sociological studies.

We can all approximate some of the reasons for the lie and the believing of the lie. If we merely look around we can appreciate that anything and everything is a potential source for self-doubt, self-hatred. Whether we were raised in a super-religious, patriarchal, alcoholic, abusive family or whether we were brought up in a loving and nurturing "spiritual" community, we might still have internalized the lie: *I am not enough.*

The point of WASH is to encourage a generative conversation. A generative conversation might feel a bit novel, a bit risky, and may hit the very nerve ("I'm not good at this!") it's examining. Generative conversations are not clear, clean, perfect conversations. They are full of Gaps, Waits, Bus Stops and the sense of "OMG, isn't there anything, anybody out there who can help me out here?" So, yes, the generative conversation may be about reaching the end of the line, not about the causes or the cures for self-hatred. We come together with another woman or women to simply affirm, "I've had enough...I'm unwilling to pay this price...There is something terribly wrong here..." and, at the same time, to refuse to make an enemy of anyone else, including ourselves.

That type of generative conversation will be difficult, maybe impossible, for a long time, at least. To come together to affirm that we are WASH, and to affirm that we will not blame others or make an enemy of ourselves, is a big commitment. With that as the foundation, what can we then talk about?

Well, let's try it and find out.

A Few Guidelines for a Generative Conversation

- Listen deeply. This means listening from the gut, not the mind.
- Adopt the attitude of a journalist or a student, listening for what you can learn, rather than for what you can agree or disagree with, or for the moment when you can jump in with your better story.
- Don't interrupt. This sounds so easy. Try it. Observe how frequently we cut one another off by intrusion.
- Sign on for a "no-fault" insurance policy with your disagreements. "Let it go" or "It's not personal" can be valuable mottoes when applied to imagined hurts or insults.
- Aim at being kind and at empowering the other person rather than being right.
- Give yourself the freedom to call time out before having to speak or answer anybody else.
- No cat pictures. Make it meaningful, make your time together (however brief) *useful.* You get the idea. You're smart. Have fun.

HIGH INTENTION FURTHERS

Don't compromise your intention by ultimately settling for a conversation or a relationship that is merely socialized and nice, although sometimes you'll have to start there. Giving a conversation or a friendship time to develop may have a huge payoff, so let it mature a bit as you ask for what you need.

There are amazingly courageous women around you. Perhaps you just haven't met them yet. No matter where you live, there are women who really want to realize their full potential as Woman. Certainly, some will not yet be ready for a climb at your altitude, but still you can enjoy them and bless them in wherever they are on the journey. Be clear about what you want, and ask for it.

You might be amazed by who shows up in your life once your intention is verbalized to the Universe (under the night sky is a good place to start). Even if you live in the desert of rural Arizona, as we do, Woman is there!

Recognize, too, that along with a good friend or two, a genuine guide, mentor, authentic spiritual teacher, or other source of help might be attracted by your cry and show up around you. (Be aware that charlatans who are looking for followers might do the same.) Be spacious and flexible enough to relax your own agenda in favor of *proven* wisdom. You'll know if the wisdom is genuine…it will feel like it comes from the inside out – of yourself! Take no one else's word for anything until you have verified it for yourself. And, as you are "testing" the resolves of prospective mentors and guides, do as my beloved spiritual teacher used to say, and so delicately, "Keep your panties on and your hand on your purse."

One serious partner in this work is better than seven or eight party gals. We have no idea how this help will show up for you, but keep praying and watching. In the meantime, work *this* program (with the exercises laid out in the book) with an imaginary friend, a woman in your own inner life. We're talking about a genuine heroine or role model you may have, but may never have met. This friend, this Woman, is someone you hold as being wise enough to be beyond the lie of *never good enough. Let this Woman love you.* Find the commonality of her love and longing in a place within yourself. Rest in her. Let her support you. Maybe she is a goddess from the Hindu pantheon. Maybe she is the Blessed Mother Mary. Maybe she is Gloria Steinem?...Patti Smith?...Maya Angelou?...Who knows? Only you can decide who inspires greatness in you beyond the lie. Make a time to "meet" with her – in your journal, or over a silent cup of tea, or during a walk in the woods. Find out what she might say or do about whatever you are exploring in yourself. Let her interrupt your life with her call to greatness and truth. If she can live outside the lie, so can you.

CONVERSATION ABOUT A DREAM

Shinay's dad Matthew led a training for an organization in which people were stuck in some ways. The employees and management were polarizing; the same tired conversations were being repeated over and over, as in "We don't have enough," "Other people aren't dedicated enough," "Our products aren't being appreciated enough," "We're not trying hard enough"... on and on.

Matthew suggested they get into conversation with each other about an initial dream they once nurtured but had forgotten. It could be a dream for the company, or an individual dream. He stressed that no Action Plans or To-Do lists were to be generated in these conversations. If action steps were drawn up afterward, it would be because folks had become connected to another person and deeply reconnected to their dreams, not because they had established more systems or planning groups.

It takes a radical leap in trust to truly comprehend what this all means. To appreciate that genuine movement and change comes about when the atmosphere is charged with the stuff of dreams! This is the opportunity you have with a friend or group. Even alone, you can do some writing about this.

What if, instead of telling stories about what is working or not working – about how many times we've failed or succeeded in circumventing *never good enough*; about how we're going to change next time – we focused the conversation with a friend on our big dreams, our heart's desires, and the possibilities that are being delayed or thwarted in life by the belief in *never good enough*?

If this sounds naïve or simplistic, it should. We don't call these "Radical Moves" for nothing. They are about the simple basics, as we've noted earlier. Can you *feel into* the difference between talking *about* self-hatred as a problem versus affirming a deep heart's desire? Talking about dreams, without apology, moves you into the state of already being beyond the limitation of self-hatred. Why not start such a conversation and learn what happens? Simply try it with no backing down because something sounds impossible or unpredictable. That's what dreams are for!

WHAT IS YOUR DREAM?

In my forties, I (Regina) learned the term *bodhichitta*, and it clicked. That became the word for the dream I'd always had, but couldn't pin down. Having a name for my dream, I was more ready, willing and able to approach it seriously. *Bodhichitta* means great love such that one dedicates oneself forever to relieve the sufferings of others. It's an impossible dream, but for me it is the only impossible dream worth living for. Life for me, now in my seventh decade of life, is more and more about caretaking my aged husband with kindness. Even though I fail at accomplishing my dream every day around him, I don't stop dreaming and aiming for it. I don't stay stuck in *not good enough*. There isn't time for me to wallow there when he is eighty-three. Like yesterday, when I got lost in needing to be right in a conversation with him. Recognizing what was happening, I got back on board (well, it took me a few hours, actually) in my best bumbling manner, but inspired by my love nonetheless. And now, writing about it, I renew that intention and hold out compassion to myself for the misstep, as I extend renewed gentleness toward him.

Reading this, Shinay says, "That's my dream, too!" I believe her.

Write about your dream:

_____

_____

_____

3

Free Your Dark Sisters

Our friend Priscilla knows something about darkness – the darker emotions like fear, rage, grief – and she talks about it often, leading those of us who know her to appreciate the invitation to "go dark" regularly, or at least from time to time. For her, terms like "underworld" and "shadow" are not just ideas; she knows her way around them, and sees her own tendencies to deny them. She genuinely loves the night, and even welcomes "bad" dreams, as painful or frightening as these can be. Dreams and dark places or experiences, she says, are teachers, unopened letters, new planets in the collective psyche, and new areas to explore in our own psyche. She doesn't deny her dark thoughts, the fact of her dark desires, or the presence of her dark sister Ereshkigal. (*Check out the myth of Inanna in the pages ahead.*)

Priscilla regularly warns us (especially the more spiritually oriented among us) of our tendencies to rise above and beyond self-hatred without first making a descent into it. She sometimes gets annoyed and frustrated by how blindly we dance forward with our enthusiasm for change. She knows this because she is frustrated with her own blindness. She begs us to hold our seat on this – to stay in place, not abandon ourselves in the face of stuff we'd rather spiritualize or deny – and to recognize that there is no easy way around or above self-hatred. We have what it takes to go into it and through it, she promises.

For me (Regina), "going through" can't mean aggressive action like ripping open old wounds. I've tried that approach for many years, and see the cost of it. I will not use any method that feels like an ice pick applied to break up the accumulated frost (or the glacial wall) around my heart. Getting to the heart's core, for me, has to be done gently, softly, and with support. By lighting even a small fire, especially in the company of those I love and those who support me, the ice begins to melt.

Melting the ice, warming the heart is a worthy goal, we believe. But it necessitates acknowledging that the ice is there. We know, as you do, that No is a common default when hard facts must be faced. We are defended against admitting the Dark, especially as it occurs in ourselves. This is understandable. It can be painful to see into defended corners. It can be painful to re-live or re-experience certain shocks and even traumas. Admittedly, this suggestion – this Radical Move – may not be the most popular. Some of us prefer to live in the upper world. Others want to avoid our darkness altogether and do yoga or go for a hike. All well and good. But if we want to deal with our self-hatred we will need to tell the raw truth about what we haven't embraced – in ourselves and others and in the world at large! Even though they are sticky, we will want to unwrap our core beliefs about *not good enough* and examine how they have been fed for years and years. We all win if we confess our "sins" – not in some greater self-hating way, but in the triumph of honest revelation. This is necessary work for all of us. Shinay and I are willing to be the Voice of Doom, as we've come to appreciate that title. As we see it, we were "doomed" without this kind of self-understanding, without this light.

A Way Out of Hell

I (Shinay) sat in the back of the van screaming into my sweatshirt. I was mad as hell. I had just tried to help pack the van for our road trip and someone had come over and told me to "Get out of the way, this is my job," and "how dare you try and do something you're no good at." *That chauvinistic pig,* I thought to myself, *how could he treat me like that!? I was only trying to help.* It was 4:30 in the morning. I was enraged, hurt, sad, exhausted, overwhelmed, and cramped in the back of a fifteen-passenger van. As I worked myself into hysterics, gasping for air, Regina looked over at me and said firmly, but gently, "Shinay, what you're experiencing is called 'hell.' You can choose to stay in hell, or get out of it. You have a choice."

I took in her words and I got "out" fast. I was not going to let my life be dictated by my rage and upset. At that point, it no longer mattered if I was right, or if he was right, or what happened. The only thing that mattered was to climb down off the ledge and regain some sense of inner balance. I'll never forget Regina's words. She was strong for me and didn't try to sugarcoat the situation. She was clear for me while I was muddled inside.

When I am able to see my darkness for what She is (which often manifests as anger, rage, explosive throw-things-at-the-wall behavior *and* deep, deep sadness for the heartbreak of the world), and I am able to just let Her *be,* the more I am able to see my anger as simply part of my whole being. This allows me a great sense of freedom. You don't need to let your Dark run the show, but you do need to acknowledge that She is present.

We give you permission to invite your Dark Sisters to tea (as Regina and Barbara will explain later in this chapter) and to relax into your own natural pulsation between light and dark. The dark aspects of our being need to be honored, just the same as the light aspects.

The Woman in the Mirror

When I (Regina) was in my early thirties, during a time of great inner stress and confusion, I spent time with a couple in southern California, staying at their home. It was a writing holiday and the opportunity to attend a conference in their town. These folks were good people, although I didn't know them well. They were friends of friends.

One afternoon, after I'd been there for about five days, I was having tea with my hostess. She asked me how I was doing, and in my habitual way I said, "Great!" Then I went on to regale her with my story about how wonderful things were going for me, how fabulous their hospitality was, and how terrific the beach was. I probably went on for five minutes when I realized that she wasn't smiling back at me. I was grinning broadly, naturally, in my own inimitable way. She was serious, however. I stopped my monologue and inquired why she had asked.

She told me that she had been parked downtown on the previous day when a young good-looking woman passed by on the sidewalk in front of her. She was struck because the woman was so attractive but looked so sad. The woman on the sidewalk didn't know she was being observed, and as she walked on a few steps she noticed her own reflection in a shop window and stopped to adjust her hair-band

48

and sunglasses. Doing that, she still lingered, staring at herself. As she did, she changed her facial expression from a flat numbness to a big smile. She adjusted her posture, and, like an actress setting foot on the stage, she flipped into the persona of a happy, free spirit.

She, the observer, noticed all these details as if watching a drama, she told me. It struck her then that this woman was deeply suffering, but couldn't let herself see it or feel it. At least not yet.

My hostess told me that this sight made her feel extremely sad. She also told me that the woman she saw downtown was me.

INANNA'S DESCENT

Inanna, the Mother Goddess from ancient Sumer, was the queen of heaven, life, and fertility, and the goddess of war and sexual love. That's quite a resume! The story of her descent into the underworld is terrifying, yet its results are ultimately transformational. She who embodies the life force will descend, deliberately; she will be stripped of her power and die, only to be reborn with a new wisdom and power.

Inanna had a sister, a part of herself, who lived in the underworld. Not only was Ereshkigal an inhabitant of the domain of death and terror, she was the absolute queen of it. She was horrifying, although beautiful; she was cruel (by our standards), although powerful. She was jealous and possessive and deceitful. With all her heavenly inspiration and knowledge, and for all her status, Inanna herself could not be saved from encountering Ereshkigal. She *had* to go into the underworld, as every woman must who wishes to be made whole. She had to confront these elemental forces of death and destruction, surrender to them, and be resurrected, sadder but wiser. There was no way around it – Inanna had to descend; otherwise she would remain forever an icon, rather than a living embodiment, the true Mother of all Creation.

Different renderings of the myth explain the reason for Inanna's visit. In one of the oldest accounts, she goes because Ereshkigal's husband has died and she wishes to attend his funeral. Rather than being pleased at such generosity, however, Ereshkigal's jealousy gets the better of her and she decides to destroy Inanna. Goodness is sometimes too painful to endure.

Inanna's descent is not a pretty one. Rather, it is a series of the most profound humiliations and tortures. Seven gates have to be passed through, and at each gate a sacrifice is demanded. One by one she is disinherited of her powers, and her entire journey becomes an initiation into darkness, pain, and loss. Not only does she relinquish her powers, but she must strip herself naked and bow low in order to enter the dark kingdom's door. Finally, she is slaughtered, her body impaled on a stake and displayed for public mockery. Here her dead body swells, the skin turns green, she rots. Completely helpless and abandoned, Inanna has no choice but to wait for redemption.

Inanna is rescued and released, yet there is no Hollywood ending to this tale. The ultimate resolution is full of consequence for Inanna, and for Ereshkigal and their male lovers – a resolution that assures a type of balance being kept in the world. Upper world can be nourished by underworld. Darkness and light must meet before they can dance.

OUR DARK SISTERS
Like Inanna, each of us has an underworld full of dark sisters. Even Mother Teresa had one! We may not want to admit this, but we all harbor dark emotions, or are plagued by them. We

hide certain behaviors and secrets, even from ourselves: we cover over painful memories; we repress and suppress all sorts of intuitive wisdom and expression; we violate our own word, discarding the promises we make to ourselves; we justify, we manipulate...you name it, we do it! We dishonor ourselves most of all by judging the underworld and its inhabitants as somehow bad or wrong or dirty or unworthy of us.

This is simply not true.

Most of the time we just don't know *what to do* with our Dark Sisters, which is why we deny them, or try to lock them up. We completely miss the point that our dark emotions are our disenfranchised sisters in need of liberation and embracing so they can do their job in waking us up. We need them, yet we dismiss their existence. They have so much to teach us, yet we turn away. They have so much to gift us with, which we throw away.

A few years ago, I (Regina) worked as a partner with a brilliant woman as we led a self-healing seminar. She was a mentor for me, and several years my senior. Her intention was pure, and I loved and admired her for this, which made the situation more challenging when I watched her interchanges with one young man in the group. In my view, her words and gestures were soaked with seduction. Anger arose in me, but I didn't want to face it because the consequences seemed too tricky. If I confronted her with my opinion, she might reject me for it; she might be deeply hurt. It might ruin our relationship, both as work partners and as friends. So I went into default mode: I immediately denied what might really be going on *by making myself wrong* – as in "mistaken" or "prudish." Women do this a lot. We make ourselves wrong for other people's breakdowns. We make ourselves wrong for failures at large – for stormy weather on the day of a picnic (after all, we *could* have chosen a covered pavilion for the event if only we'd been omniscient); for traffic jams on the highway (after all, we *did* have a moment's intuitive flash that taking a back road or leaving ten minutes earlier would have been good to do today); for our kids' getting sick. Name your way.

In the case I'm referring to, this self-blame festered only so long. Then it evolved into dissatisfaction with my life circumstances in general. I became annoyed by our seminar and found that it wasn't fun anymore. I had fantasies of driving away in the middle of the night, leaving behind anyone or anything that might cause such disruptive feelings. I wondered what my husband would say if I suggested moving to Lapland.

The running-away program changed swiftly to aggressive desires: I wanted her actions revealed to all, blatantly, so that she would have to suffer the consequences; I wanted her to be punished, leaving me vindicated. These are painful admissions, yet I confess them here because they are common human responses to any perceived threat. By owning them for what they are – thoughts, feelings, fantasies – and simply telling the truth about their existence, I'm pointing myself toward a possible way out.

This evolution of moods and emotions in me (from discomfort to aggression) didn't take weeks, it took hours. I was lost and sad and angry, all in the space of an afternoon and an evening. I was suffering…big time, and that's *always* a clue and a cue. I was "lost in the underworld" and needed help. Luckily, I know a bit about such dark places. Luckily, I recognized that these Dark Sisters (denial, self-blame, withdrawal, desire for revenge) are only mind trips and emotional blips, but trips and blips that could, rightly used, actually become allies for me.

So I took a deep breath. I created space in my chest and mind and belly. I relaxed a little. I asked myself if I had the courage to confront my friend directly. I didn't. I asked myself if I was willing to step into the mess, without being aggressive toward myself or to her. I wasn't. I asked myself if I could let it go, and let her come to this recognition for herself, in her own time, and in her own way, if such was actually needed. I was. I asked myself if I could let her be imperfect, or even seductive (God help us!), and instead trust in the love that I remembered was at the core of her intentions, as it was of mine. I did. I asked myself if I was willing to ride the wave of this turmoil of thoughts and emotions, simply observing them, without having to do anything about them. I was! I embraced my own Dark Sisters of righteous anger, denial, justification, fear, and let them know that I heard them, but didn't need to express them.

On the last day of the workshop, we met to share our assessment of the program and my friend asked me directly if I had any feedback or help to offer her. By this time I was no longer charged by my own reactivity to her behavior and was able to tell her what I saw. She honored me with deep listening and offered some feedback (which I invited) on my participation that I could use, too.

Certainly I was free to believe in my mind and emotions! Not a good option. I was free to turn away, shocked and disgusted, from this situation without saying a word. Also not the best plan! I was free to cut this woman out of my life. Ouch! But I knew that without attempting to deal with mind and emotions on the spot, this event would stick to me and cause ongoing suffering, even if I never saw her again. I knew that this same situation would arise with somebody else, probably sooner rather than later. I knew that what was unworked or denied would hurt, and that what was unworked or denied would generate greater self-hatred. I didn't want to do that.

The key in this case was to deal with the dark in *myself*, not to try to change it in her.

Interestingly, when I am able to tell the truth about what I judge as "the dark" in myself, and if I am courageous enough to share this with a sister or two, I elicit relief and even gratitude from them. Ever notice that? When I admitted to another friend that I lusted after a young man half my age in one of my seminars in Europe, we both laughed in the recognition of the power hidden in releasing dark secrets. When Janet told me and a few other women-friends about her two abortions, the group of us spontaneously embraced her, holding her pain and loving her all the more. When Debbie revealed that she secretly rejoiced at another woman's failure, those in her confidence talked about their own "evil wishes."

Many women are afraid of such dark truth telling because they anticipate being lost in the pain. They fear that talking – or even thinking – about it will strengthen their self-hatred and shame. While it might seem logical that one thing leads to another, this is not necessarily the case. Such denied cancers can often metastasize. Such undisclosed wounds and self-judged sins can precipitate bigger wounds and "sins" to further preoccupy our time. Without such self-observation (without telling the truth, to ourselves at least, by observing the whole range of our feelings), we easily dull the edge of conscience and can end up sadder and no wiser despite our advancing age.

I know there is redemptive value in vulnerability, in honest self-disclosure. As Jean Valjean understood in *Les Miserables*, admitting a lie might bring condemnation from the world, but not admitting it would bring ultimate damnation to his own soul, to say nothing of his future life. It takes enormous courage to bear the pain of one's own failings (real or imagined) and to expose them to the healing light of God's mercy, which is genuine self-compassion. It takes great courage to speak of our "dark" with other sisters of mercy. So often, what we think is some unique form of negativity or darkness is actually the common fare of others. Just knowing that is useful, and moves us ahead in this intention to view self-hatred (our Dark Sister) with genuine compassion.

THE HONORED GUEST AT YOUR TABLE

My (Regina's) sweet and wise mentor-mother, Barbara, once used the phrase "honored guest at your table" with me when I asked her help with some debilitating fears. Instead of going to battle with my fears (of death, of airplane travel, of doing something wrong...I have lots of them), Barbara advised inviting them to tea and asking them, like friends, what they were needing and what they had to give.

I went a step further. I imagined my fears as characters in a royal court by giving them regal names: Lady Turbulence, Her Royal Highness Queen Death, the Duchess of Perfection. Then I invited one or more of them to have tea with me, using fantasy visualization or, more specifically, by writing a dialogue with the character in my journal. This opened the conversation.

Giving our Dark Sisters a lovely title is one way to break a pattern with them. I used this approach with fears, but any aspect of ourselves that we would rather deny is perfect material for this royal treatment: jealousy, overeating, bossiness, shaming of others, anger, competitiveness. Talking kindly to the "Lady" or the "Queen" actually confuses the character into momentarily, at least, relaxing her grip – physically, mentally, and emotionally.

Shinay and I can attest that we *do know* the way out of some varieties of self-hatred based in our dark emotions. We've merely forgotten. When we can call jealousy a "Lady," we can drop the label of "enemy," as if she is somehow a separate stranger instead of an old family friend. Jealousy, we might imagine, keeps hanging around because she's desperate to be heard. She has something invaluable for us, something to teach us. Instead, most of us will fight with her; we justify or resist or hide our jealousy, and make ourselves bad for it. Jealousy could be an honored guest at our table if we didn't immediately start kicking her so hard, or making excuses for her.

Shinay and I can't predict what *your* Lady or Queen will tell you if you invite her as an honored guest to your table, or what precisely she may ask for, but we do know that this simple act of release can be useful, and the information might be surprising.

I made these notes about my growing relationship with Lady Fear, who continually shows up on my airplane trips.

Fear of Flying

I (Regina) have NOT overcome my fear of flying, but when I asked Fear to come to me as a Lady, as a friend, she told me a secret that somehow changed everything. One day, as we bounced into the airport in Bucharest, she told me that she wasn't going away, ever, but that didn't mean I couldn't use her as *a reminder to love myself anyway*, in all kinds of circumstances.

When fighting with Fear, I was also hating myself for not winning, not overcoming. Women like me (especially those on a spiritual path) are not supposed to be bothered by such "small" fears. We're supposed to trust in God, surrender, relax, and attend to the needs of others above ourselves. When I couldn't do that, I'd hate myself more. I'd work harder. I was getting worse instead of better the older I got.

Now, *I watch it all arise*: the contracted belly, the sweaty palms, the thoughts of falling from the sky, the prayers for salvation mixed with songs and chants, the images of burning wreckage, my husband's face, the sounds of crying babies. I watch it all and note the sensations produced in the body.

"I love you anyway, and will love you no matter what you suggest or what pictures you send up," I say to my mind. "I love you anyway," I say to my belly and hands. "I love you through it all," I say to my trembling chest. "I forgive you and love you, and accept never getting it right," I say to all the parts and parcels here. "I will always love you," I say again, even if I don't entirely believe it. But saying it works so much better than its opposite, which is spiraling down into more fear and self-loathing.

Important note: This *doesn't* make the fear go away. The point is, it shifts something. Instead of trying to *stop* what is, I *use* what is to learn something about how mind works, how body responds, how love moves, how breath flows. Focusing on self-love and self-honoring has become a preoccupation that seems to be strengthening a different set of pathways in my brain. I suspect it is making some difference with that persistent self-hatred that Shinay and I have been talking about.

This little vignette contains a seed of wisdom that we want to plant in your garden, too. We pointed to the wisdom of placing attention (and intention) in Radical Move 1. The seed is this: *Wherever you place your attention, your life force will follow.* By moving attention from the fear, if only for a moment at a time, and placing it on self-acceptance (or on the body, the breath), the life force moves there.

And this is not all. You don't have to be successful in keeping your attention riveted on the new thing, the new place, the new attitude. You only have to intend it, generally, and do it when you can. The life force is intelligent. It wants you to thrive. Make Life Force your sister, as Rita did in the following story.

Rita's Story

No matter what I have accomplished in my life thus far, it has never been good enough. Relationships, work, art, parenting...not good enough! I've often wondered how this happened. Where did this story come from, and why have I allowed it to continue to permeate every aspect of my existence, creating suffering, depression and darkness?

Recently, I found some old photos of myself, pictures in which I am clearly less affected by years of this false belief. In one of my favorites, I am about three and standing in my parents very '50s-style den holding my sister's hand. It's summertime, birthday time, and we're dressed for the picture with ribbons in our hair and matching rose-colored jumpers. I stare undaunted into the camera. Directly in front of us is a hassock with a sheet cake sitting on it. It's our birthday cake, and we are both very excited about it. A very special cake, with twin Barbie dolls on top, standing side by side. Their dresses are made of icing.

Lately, almost daily, I've been gazing at the picture as a form of practice. My "younger self" clearly has much to tell me about basic goodness and quiet presence. The more I stare at the picture the more I see someone who is comfortable in her skin, alive in her knowing, and awake in her essence and radiance. She is powerful, confident, and alive.

Using that earlier version of myself in a directed way is starting to affect me positively. That "little girl" is my own true self – eternal, unchanging, beautiful, pure. Free.

She's not a people pleaser, afraid of being inadequate or not PC. She's just being and moving through her life in a very essential, organic way. "She" has been there all along, advising me, coaching me, loving me. "She" is "me," and I just haven't been seeing and listening. The more I begin to embrace that we are indeed the same "person," the lighter I feel.

Can it really be that simple? Can this lifelong sentence of sadness and feelings of ineptitude simply vanish by an inner knowing? I believe it can! What is required is revolutionary. I must continue the practice of gazing regularly at the picture, remember my own true self, love the lessons of the lie, and see the lie for the strategy of survival that it is/ was. Through daily practice of compassion for myself and renewed intention to honor the truth, I begin to replace the old negative habit of "not good enough."

THE WORK OF BIG SPACE

As we venture into the domain of darkness, we are sometimes navigating a thin bridge over a deep chasm. Without guidance and some support in the form of gentleness, forgiveness, and acceptance from friends, sisters or mentors, it may be easy for us to turn back, or to slip on the edge as we admit our pains and failings. Some of us will require the help of a trained therapist, as specific trauma work is more than our own friends can do for us. But we can use our friends as support to move us in that direction and perhaps to give us recommendations for individual help if it becomes clear that this is needed.

Exposing my painful "dark" to the light of my sister's presence might begin with speaking my failings, my doubts, my fears and anxieties, with no comment from others, and the spacious silence of a compassionate heart. Shinay and Nancy and other sisters are willing to give this to me – what I call "Big Space." In the last chapter, in speaking of our friend Cecilia, we called it "deep listening." This is offering breathing room and a mood of tenderness to whatever is offered. Big Space is the opposite of immediate advice or consolation, which are easy and cheap. The expansive uncertainty of Big Space is a lot more challenging. It means choosing to take the long view of human development and the big embrace of "just doing the best I can."

Deliberate and conscious breathing, with alternately expanding and relaxing lungs and diaphragm, can provide an entry into Big Space. We are advocates for this – before, during, and after any sharing sessions. Visualization is also useful for some. "Imagine putting soft flesh on the arms of Great Mother and crawling into her lap," Regina suggested to Marion, a suffering friend, "telling her what you feel bad about." This relaxation, along with conscious breathing, encourages us to rest in the pain and the imperfection of human life.

EXERCISE – "Big Space" Breathing

I (Shinay) use this breathing exercise (simplified here) in my yoga classes regularly as well as in my day-to-day life. It's a way to soothe the nerves, remove phlegm, give endurance, and tone the entire system. It can be done anytime, anywhere, even with your eyes open. For details on this specific technique see *Light on Yoga* by B.K.S. Iyengar. This exercise is called *Ujjayi Pranayama*. *Ujjayi* in Sanskrit means "triumphantly uprising or victorious." This is the process of finding Big Space on the inside, for your body and your mind.

1. Sit in a comfortable position with your spine straight and your diaphragm free. (Sit either on the edge of a chair/couch or on the edge of a cushion on the floor.)

2. Place one hand on your belly and one hand over your chest.

3. Exhale fully.

4. Take a slow, deep, steady breath in through both nostrils and fill the belly first, moving the air up to the collarbones. As B.K.S. Iyengar explains, "The passage of the incoming air is felt on the roof of the palate and makes a sibilant sound (*sa*). This should be heard."

5. Fill the lungs all the way up. Taking care not to bloat the abdomen when inhaling, pull the abdomen back toward the spine.

6. Exhale slowly, deeply, and steadily from the collarbones down to the pubic bone until the lungs are completely empty. The brushing of the air on the upper palate should make an aspirant sound (*ha*).

7. As you breathe, concentrate on taking deeper and fuller breaths, elongating your inhale and exhale. Keep track of your breath by using a count of six or eight for both the inhale and the exhale so they are the same length of duration. You may also wish to use a mantra, a chant or the words *hum* and *sah*. *Hum* on the inhale and *sah* on the exhale. This will help to train the mind as well as focus your attention solely on your breath.

8. Do this several times. Then, after an exhale, return to your natural breathing.

9. B.K.S. Iyengar says, "This is the only pranayama [breathing exercise] that can be done at all times of the day and night."

WHAT THE DARK TEACHES

Keep in mind that we are not revealing our darkness to ourselves or to each other in order to do away with it. We need the dark. My (Regina's) own dark virtues, my sins, my failings, my "negative" emotions, my grasping ignorance are bands of my full-spectrum life. Even if I don't immediately understand how these dark bands can be valuable, as I relax around them, embrace them (this doesn't mean flaunt them), bring gentle forgiveness and tenderness to them – without trying to change or do something about them – they start to reveal their own illusory reality as well as their own unique power.

Our friend Rachel used her grief to let her love out. Rachel is three years younger than Shinay, and a friend to both of us. Her mom died when Rachel was only nine years old, and Shinay affirms that Rachel never fully grieved. ("I know, I was there with her," Shinay attests.) Rachel's mom had cancer, so it was not a sudden death, but at that age Rachel was asked to deal with stuff a nine-year-old doesn't normally have to face.

Five or six years after the death, Rachel started a project and named it after her mom – *SITA*, she called it. Rachel developed a support group dedicated to helping teens move through their own grief. Consistently, Rachel held these meetings once a week, even if no one else showed. She used her grief to move with, through, and even a bit beyond the darkness. She made herself available to the suffering of teens everywhere. She confronted her personal sadness and used it to let her love out.

We live in a culture that denies the dark. Even as we are obsessed with darkness in the media (read the news, look at the offerings of movies, follow a political debate), we don't want to face it in ourselves. Everything is put "out there"; no responsibility is put "in here." Living with open eyes (and remaining bright) in a dark-denying culture is hard work. We need our friends to help keep us clear and honest; to keep reminding us of our basic goodness; to keep urging us to take responsibility for how life shows up around us. We need to keep telling the hard truths without wallowing in any kind of self-pity or masochism.

Kind, Kind, Kind

I (Shinay) am an advocate for living life to the *fullest* (whatever that means), accepting what is, being kind kind kind, and loving myself.

This evening I was none of those things. I was pinched, contracted, and totally stressed out. I was a scared little girl who felt unloved and could not muster any motivation to feel adequate. I was believing "the lie."

I was set to teach yoga at 5:30 p.m. and it was too late to call in sick. I got dressed for class and drove to the studio trying not to cry because then I'd have puffy eyes and my mascara would run down my face. All I could do was pray that no one showed up for class. Five people came. I was depressed. What did I do?

I sat there...at the front of the room, with all eyes turned on me. Five expectant students, each one relying on her weekly yoga class to inspire and uplift her. There was nowhere to go but forward. So I opened my mouth and spoke (to myself, and to them) about the importance of self-love and accepting *what is* in the moment without judgment, regardless of what I might be feeling or thinking (and I certainly wasn't feeling or thinking the love in that moment!). Still, I spoke about opening up to the support we need, and about finding help in the arms of love, meditation, and yoga asana (the physical postures).

Despite trying to hold back my own tears, and wrestling with the incongruity of my own state, I managed to get through the class. While I often judge myself a hypocrite when I can't be "on" all the time, I also know that I can access a place deeper than feelings or thoughts, and speak from there.

We will all forget at times. There will be moments, days, weeks or years during which we just need to keep moving forward, even if we don't fully believe (that is, think or feel) that we are enough. The only way to move beyond is to just keep going, and to tell the truth to ourselves as we go.

There can be gold in feeling "not good enough." Believe it or not! But we have to mine it. While self-hatred is generally a result of a neurotic lie, a grand illusion in the mind that we have accepted as true, it may also be the result of seeing (and feeling) the gap between our truest heart wishes and our stumbling attempts – failed actions in support of those wishes. *Feeling* our unfulfilled potential is golden. *Sensing* the pain and suffering of the world and our own inability to address it – this is golden. *Observing* how often we take the easy way out, how we hold ourselves back, how we overlook the opportunity to love, this is pure gold! We can allow ourselves to be bothered by this pain; we can let it stay untouched for some time; we can hold on in the dark, allowing our pain to gestate in order to release its transformational potential. Attempting to fix it, trying to forget it, obsessing about it, or judging it as something bad builds the foundation for the next level of self-hatred. Don't do it.

Courage!

Can you let your "dark" really bother you, for a while at least, without starting a new cause to counteract it? The recognition of a dulled conscience and repeated failings can be a fruitful darkness, one that provokes deep consideration and deep discomfort. Living with this pain, this incompleteness, this sense of inadequacy ultimately connects us with the rest of the world. (Or did you think you were the only one in pain?) The recognition of the world's catastrophe is one way of contextualizing your own paltry self-hatred. Darkness does heal things.

We wish we could give you some easy formula for "going dark" and promise you bright skies in only ten days. But we cannot and will not. What we can and must do is beg you not to leave your own dark, the dark of your sisters, and the dark of the world out of your work here. What we will do as we proceed is continue to address the nature of mind, which is where darkness gets generated, and suggest ways to work with it. Writing will be an invaluable tool in moving from denial to revelation, and from revelation to forgiveness.

Grace intervenes in the lives of the highly intentioned. It really does.

EXERCISE – A Dialogue with a Dark Sister

Introduction: This exercise is best done in a personal journal, or simply by writing it out on paper, or on your computer. However, it could also be done alone by recording yourself in conversation with the imagined Dark Sister. It could also be spoken in the presence of a truly caring, nonjudgmental friend (but, decidedly, that is harder).

GET TO KNOW YOUR SISTER

1. Decide which sister to dialogue with. You probably have several Dark Sisters hanging around. Decide on one to start with. She may not be the most prominent, or the most "wicked" or troublesome, so give yourself permission to start with whoever wants to talk: Fear, Anxiety, Jealousy, Comparison, Dissatisfaction, Lateness, Procrastination…it's up to you.

2. Give her a royal title and dress her up. You can choose how to refer to her, and how she will look. A clue here: because you think of her as "dark" you should go out of your way to make her an honored guest; otherwise, she may simply reject your invitation. Give her a noble title – Queen, Blessed, Lady, Mother – even if you don't immediately feel her nobility. Pretending is good here! Then imagine how she is dressed to fit her noble name. What is she wearing? What does her face look like? Her eyes? What color is her skin? Is she wearing jewelry or carrying anything? It's up to you.

If you don't follow our suggestions because "she" seems to insist on a name or an appearance that differs from ours, trust your own lead. We are simply using our own experience and intuition, but yours is precious too!

3. Write out her name, description, and life story. Before you begin your conversation with her, write out briefly what she is called and what she looks like. (You're making this up, don't be afraid.) Be as specific as you wish to be. We have found that the more detail we use, the more interesting the conversation becomes.

Take a few minutes to write out a brief biography of her. Make it up! Where and when was she born? (*Lady Fear entered the Royal Court of ME in 1949 when I was four years old and we moved to New York City from the countryside.*) What has been her life experience? How has she occupied herself over the years of her life? (*She's constantly in motion, running ahead of me to be there when I try to smooth out all the bumps so she can capitalize on my imbalance. She waits in the corner of every room as I manipulate any and every situation to help me avoid confrontation. When that fails, she laughs her high-pitched laugh.*)

4. Take it slowly. Recognize that this exercise might take much more time than you originally thought and that it might be enormously revealing in an archetypal sort of way. If this step is enough, stop here and come back to the Dialogue part on another good day.

5. The dialogue. Now that you have a sense of your tea companion, welcome her to your table and begin writing a dialogue with her. Let her reply to your questions, in her own way, in her own good time. Well, of course, you'll know that you are making it all up. No problem. We also "make up" suffering and stories that don't serve us. Use this opportunity to let one of your many inner "I"s speak to you in a way that may surprise you. Be open, be gentle. Listen.

(continued on next page)

6. Concluding. When you've had enough for this writing session, even if you feel incomplete, thank your sister for her time and say goodbye. Make a date for another tea together, if that seems like a good idea.

Slowly read back what you've written. Don't rush it. Now write a little conclusion for yourself: "As a result of this dialogue, I…" and write whatever you have learned or whatever strikes you as significant.

If you wish, use your meeting with your friend or friends as a way to share with another person what you are learning and seeing.

Delight Yourself

People who are full of delight are delightful to be with. And, *bonus*, the atmosphere of delight is mostly too thin for self-hatred to flourish in. But trying to stop the thoughts and feelings of self-hatred is usually the wrong aim because the old adage proves true. "What we resist persists." Fighting, battling, warring with, stamping out, obliterating self-hatred is not the paradigm we subscribe to. Shinay and I are about setting a fire within, cultivating enthusiasm for what delights us, and venturing into domains of new potential delights, new forms of self-expression. We're about melting self-hatred with this inner fire, not hacking at it with that proverbial ice-axe. We are about focusing our precious attention on what brings joy, delight, satisfaction, and letting the self-hatred take a back seat.

This is where we start.
We cultivate the things that delight us,
and we grow bigger than the moods that possess us,
like self-hatred. And…well…who knows?

Delight isn't highlighted nearly enough in the adult world! When it is used, it's too much, too loosely, as in some advertisement that urges you to delight your senses with the latest hair product. But the delight that children exhibit, the delight that shines in their eyes on a Christmas morning, or when a new pet enters their world, or a much loved person unexpectedly appears in the room – this isn't often our daily fare. And why not?

Although "delight" in English comes from the root *delectare* – to entice, in Latin – and has to do with pleasure or joy, Shinay and I are just as interested in the obvious word "light" that it contains. As in, "I've seen de' light!" Laugh if you wish, but hear us out on this one.

When someone says, "You light up my life," they are offering the highest compliment. When there is a discernible light in someone's eyes, we know they are on a love quest, not some passing fad or fancy. When the great spiritual traditions of the world speak about the ultimate Light, they are speaking about a Force at the core of creation, the essence of the creative process. What turns on the light in *your* world? And what (if anything) is the more ultimate Light that you seek?

Being honest, some of us are willing to admit to participating in a conspiracy *against* joy and delight. Some of us have a terror of it, in fact. For those of us raised in a religious or spiritual tradition, and even those who have adopted a revised version of such, inwardly we may be afraid of too much happiness, too much success, too much blessing. We haven't earned the right to be delighted, to be happy, we mistakenly surmise, especially since others are suffering so much. And even if we have some delight, it certainly can't last! (Well, this is true, too, but that's another subject.) We dread the disappointment when it leaves; or we're afraid that punishment or deprivation is bound to follow. Didn't our parents warn us that if we got too excited, too worked up, we'd be crying soon enough? Such self-defeating programs are deeply embedded in the culture. No wonder we have them, too.

When our good friend Celeste fell in love at age sixty and was honored as a much-desired partner and lover by a wonderful man, she also shook with fear. She kept asking us, "How did I deserve this?" Was it a setup for a future letdown? She needed our affirmation that she was good enough to be loved so much. We assured her that she was, and that regardless of the outcome of the relationship, she is worthy of great light, great love, because that is who she is essentially. She bravely let us touch this place of insecurity in her. It took courage on her part (*coeur* in French means heart) to risk such vulnerability. It took courage on our parts to tell the truth as we saw it, reminding her of her basic goodness and dignity. We en-*cour*-aged her.

So this might be a good place to begin to engage your friend or sisters about how as much as we applaud the value of joy we still fear it. We even defend against it: as in refusing to receive a compliment without some apology or excuse, or in discounting the price we pay in terms of our own "gross personal happiness" and that of those around us by forever following a path of reasoned sensibility and act-your-age-ness.

In this chapter we will argue for grown-up-woman delight as opposed to silly indulgence masquerading as happiness. To begin, we suggest you consider the costly sacrifice of life force that follows when a self-centered focus on being appropriate, on being "good," continually trumps the spontaneity of play.

WANNA PLAY?

Children play. If left alone, some of them will play unendingly, or until they are too hungry to go on. Or they will play until they become suddenly frightened and need some reassurance. They play with enthusiasm, without any judgment of themselves.

The two ten-year-old girls playing outside my (Regina's) dining room window are currently involved in an epic drama in which their army of smurf-trolls are capturing and tying up their Barbies, dipping them into the birdbath, and then imprisoning them in a bramble hut for some future adventure. The Barbies, meanwhile, are plotting their escape, unbeknownst to the trolls. The dialogue is nonstop: "And pretend that the trolls don't know...and then we'll...and then pretend..."

I'll come back in an hour and see what success has been achieved. But I won't let them know I'm observing, because that type of interruption is bound to be tinged with some horror on my part about the cruelty of the game. God help us, but adults do this to children all the time. No wonder we don't know how to play. This judging and manipulating was visited upon us, and we simply pass it on, little realizing how we are killing the very enthusiasm that could lead to something we can't even imagine. Enthusiasm opens doors. New possibilities emerge. This apparently cruel play (from an adult perspective) might inspire a crusade of warrior Barbies, or a peace pact the likes of which we've never known. Or, it might get really terrible. But these girls are *playing*, and currently no one and nothing is being harmed – except the sensibilities of well-meaning but ignorant adults.

The point is, we don't know *where* such enthusiasm will take them, or us, and that's why it is such a great prize. It is time to revisit the domains of enthusiasm in our own lives and allow them to be celebrated. Sadly, however, some of us have moved so far away from the dharma of delight that we don't know anymore what *would* delight us, what *does* delight us. That's why we've got friends and sisters. That's why we are making a few Radical Moves.

Dedicate yourself to the good you deserve and desire for yourself. Give yourself peace of mind. You deserve to be happy. You deserve delight.
    – Hannah Arendt

Beauty does not linger; it only visits. Yet beauty's visitation affects us and invites us into its rhythm; it calls us to feel, think and act beautifully in the world: to create and live a life that awakens the Beautiful. A life without delight is only half a life.
    – John O'Donohue

The capacity for delight is the gift of paying attention.
    – Julia Margaret Cameron

It is a pleasure to wonder at the mystery we are and find delight in the vastness of reality that is embedded in our beings.
    – Krista Tippett

Once we believe in ourselves we can risk curiosity, wonder, spontaneous delight, or any experience that reveals the human spirit.
    – e.e. cummings

THE BODY OF DELIGHT

Delight is a slightly different flavor of love than happiness or inner peace or fulfillment. Delight is something that the *body knows*, only occasionally backed up by the mind's logic. Delight within the body is a soft, tender sense of loving what you love. Delight speaks to us from the cells of the womb, from the hair on our arms, from the soles of our feet, from the tip of our tailbone, from the relaxation of facial features.

It says to us, "I deeply appreciate *this*...whatever it is – *this* piece of sushi; *this* bittersweet longing; *this* aroma of sandalwood; *this* moment of waiting for you at the airport; *this* raw song by Bob Dylan; *this* person whom I barely know; *this* piece of music that I can hear in the distance."

Delight gets cultivated by listening/feeling into what makes the body hum...not necessarily by focusing on what satisfies the mind (although feeding the mind with great poetry and other sources of wisdom will bring delight to the body as well). Learning what delights *you* is a challenge because we've accepted the culture's designation of "good" stuff and "bad" stuff. We don't expect that everyone will have the same degree of clarity about what delights them. It takes time to learn what makes the body hum. But, without giving it attention, a person could spend a lifetime and miss it.

We'll have more to say about the delight of the body in the next Radical Move, "Inhabit Your Body." But for now, it is important to make this distinction early on so you can be enjoying yourself as you read on. Attune yourself to your breath, right now. Sense your whole body, right now. Relax your body, right now. Thank you.

WHERE'S *YOUR* BARRY MANILOW?

A woman (let's call her Jackie) whom I (Regina) much respect told me about an adventure she had in inviting Barry Manilow to perform for a benefit concert for the homeless in New York City. He accepted. He sang the songs that Jackie most loved. The concert yielded a huge return for the cause, and the whole event hit the bell at the top of her own private delight scale. Jackie now tells her story enthusiastically, reminding her listeners that they, too, can trust their delight light. She reports that when she was scheduling the event, she regularly needed to defend her choice of Manilow as her big talent, as many of her closest friends and most sophisticated associates thought that, in their most humble opinion, he was just too schmaltzy and sentimental. They had big personal judgments about Barry Manilow's music and didn't hesitate to share them, albeit humorously (and condescendingly).

Jackie was unperturbed. She's like that! She loves Manilow's style, his music, his voice, and she refuses to apologize for her taste. Whether it's inviting Barry Manilow to a benefit concert or buying orange pumps that won't go with any current outfit, she tries to let delight guide her choices. Jackie is not only a highly successful woman, she is also great to be around. People are delighted in her company.

How about you? Are there secret delights you haven't allowed yourself to share with another person, much less actually accomplished? Are there potential delights you've put off because you imagine they are too expensive to pursue? Too risky to practice? Too silly in the eyes of the world around you? Maybe all you need is a co-conspirator to move you in that direction. Anyone you know?

Are there colors you love but never wear? Are there picnics you've been postponing? Are there solo retreats you long for? Flower-arranging classes or icon-painting workshops to attend? Poetry readings to give or go to? The lists are endless. What are we waiting for?

Doing *Nothing* and Staring at the Wall

"Our delight is not going to be cultivated by *doing* more," Shinay declared from her hospital bed when, at age twenty-three, she returned from Europe with pneumonia. She was leveled. When I showed up in her room, despite her occasional struggles for breath, she was both exhausted and delighted. It is possible to be delighted and still endure a headache, or even a major illness, we agreed. What about sitting with boredom until doing *nothing* actually becomes delightful? we enquired. I'd done this many times during solitary retreat. Until I determined to "just do nothing," I had no reference point for the delight of doing nothing.

I will admit it, doing nothing is not easy. But there is probably no quicker and more effective path to self-understanding than the attempt. The caveat, however, is that the doing nothing must have no judgment attached, which includes having no judgment about the judgment about "wasting time and being totally useless" that will arise. And it will arise, count on it. Still, it may prove to be worth the non-effort!

A Radical Suggestion

Take a day for nothing. Don't go anywhere. Don't plan anything. No expectations for any accomplishment. Put coverings over your mirrors. Turn off your phone (or put a message on it that says, "Day of Delight happening, call tomorrow"). Unplug your computer. Put a *Do Not Disturb* sign on your front door. Dress in your most comfortable clothes. Put a bunch of simple pickup foods in one corner of your kitchen and resist the temptation to snack on others. Do nothing, either indoors or outside. But feel free to relocate as the urge arises. Enjoy the nothing.

ART AND ECSTASY

We want you all to cultivate your art, whether that art is painting or sculpture, writing, cake-making, or exotic orchids. Art can become a source of delight and even ecstasy. It's a source of food that your body is craving. Art is about generativity, and generativity is soul food, one of the qualities of an enlivened inner life, which is a sure route beyond self-hatred.

In our own not-so-humble opinion, real change has more to do with ecstasy or delight than with trying harder and being a super heroine about your life's work. The best practice might just be the cultivation of "a-Muse-ment," or delight, or ecstasy – a very heady and enormously regenerative wine that is essentially given from Above. (It's a mystery, so – believe us – you'll waste a lot of time if you try to figure it out.) Ecstasy is accessed by opening to emptiness, to not-knowing, to longing, to gentle regard, to honesty, humility, childlikeness, and many other similar virtues. Any artist of merit will tell you the same. He or she doesn't know *where* or *how* they are able to do what they do, despite the years of training they may have undertaken. The training is only what they do to refine the instrument, but the communication of the music, the color, the form, the word that moves the heart...well, these are *given* and *freely* to the deserving trainee by the Muse, the Lord, the Love, the Divine, the Goddess, the great and abiding Mystery.

We want you to invite ecstasy and delight at every turn – and that may require that you put aside the time, establish a place, and narrow down to a single method, or two, and let yourself express your art, which is another way to speak about the passion of your *being*!

The reason we are self-hating is that this "not enough" default fills in the gaps when we aren't *being*. Therefore, we encourage ourselves, and you, to cultivate genuine delight and ecstasy, not self-indulgent highs (through too much food, alcohol, or any other addictive substance) or flitting distractions (going from one party, hobby, relationship, or fun thing to another). Self-hating diminishes in proportion to our commitment to *being*.

A HARD ROAD, TOO

In describing our delights, it may be necessary to get past the easy stuff – like a vacation in Hawaii, a trip to a spa, a night on the town – and allow ourselves to consider the harder, long-haul stuff that feeds our souls at the essence level.

Shinay and I have a woman-friend, Clare, who has climbed Mt. McKinley. She is, in fact, training for Everest. The climbing is her delight and, as she freely admits, it is also hell. She took me out one day to the climbing wall at the small town gym, implored me to squeeze my oversized feet into shoes that were deliberately two sizes too small, and strapped me up. Clare knew that I hurt, but she also knew the possibility such hurting held. I admit that through the experience I, too, glimpsed what this degree of focus and discipline might mean for setting my intentions in other domains.

Shinay's 300-Mile Bike Trip

There's nothing like a body, a bike, and the open road to spell *freedom* and *delight* for Shinay. It was December, just after dawn, and I stamped my feet to keep the blood flowing. I would warm up once I got on my bicycle and started peddling, but at the moment I was just trying to get feeling back into my fingers so I could zip my saddle bags and get on the road. My friend Lisa and I had spent the night outside Sierra Vista, Arizona, at an altitude of almost 5,000 feet. It was C-O-L-D. We could see our breath as we laughed together over the ice crystals that had formed on the *inside* of our tent. The water bottles we had stuck in the bottom of our sleeping bags were also frozen. The only thing we had for breakfast that morning was the rest of the Oreo cookies we bought at Big Lots and a few spoonfuls of almond butter. "Let's get the hell out of here!" Lisa exclaimed. I couldn't agree more.

It was my hair-brained idea to ride our bicycles 300 miles around southern Arizona from Tucson to Bisbee, through Patagonia, and back to Tucson for a week in December during our holiday break. I've never been so tired or sore or in love with my body in my entire life. I've also never felt so connected to my physical body as a powerful, sustaining force of energy. Ever. I've done a lot of other strenuous outdoor activities in my life, but this was something entirely different.

During that week, although we had a schedule to keep that was stressful at times because we had to ride no matter what, I was in love with body, bike and the open road. Immense delight came from knowing my body was being used and is useful. I was not merely existing, I was energy in motion, getting from one place to another with the power of my thighs. There was delight in being outside. Delight in having nothing to do but pedal all day long. Delight in eating whatever I wanted because a few hours later it would all be burned up. Delight in sore muscles, aching butt bones, and wind-burned skin. Delight in accomplishment. This was being a woman. This was power. This was being alive. This was hard work and the reward of knowing that I did it and I could do it again.

I didn't even train.

Admit it! We know that some of you *like* weathering a storm. Some of us actually *love* to walk in the intense wind, or in the rain, or to trudge through snow; to camp out and build a fire. Our friend Andi works with the dying and their families; this is her delight. Amethyst is fueled by the excruciating exactitude of traditional icon painting. Jana finds her delight in the intense practice she endures as a pianist with a local symphony. Josie is overjoyed by the world of art she finds amidst recycled materials.

Consider this: some resistance and some difficulty is generally inherent in any activity that causes delight. But when we are really deriving delight from something, we don't let resistance stop us. Resistance can actually be a sign that we are on the right track toward a worthwhile goal. Shinay and I suggest that you pass a resolution within your own house stating, "Delight and resistance are good friends. Let them co-exist."

Commit yourself to a delight quotient that is mature, grown up, whatever the weather. Encourage your sisters to join you in this. Remember that wimpy women, complainers and dabblers are a real drag to deep-delight work, so determine to stalk (search out and identify) these inclinations in yourself. Dabblers can be dangerous because they get all excited one day and then never show up again. We all have dabbler instincts. Just keep them in conscious awareness. And curb your enthusiasm for the quick fix. These Radical Moves are not so hard, but they do take time. Delight yourself, and observe what happens.

Shinay and I are here to testify that delight is a counterpoint to self-hatred, and that cultivating delight is an operant key to entering this breakthrough state in which we trust and appreciate ourselves and each other. We're advocates for a dharma of delight – a wisdom teaching that advances joy and fulfillment as the antidote to self-hatred.

Let delight shine.

Delighting Others

Are you delighted when you can send a gift to someone whom you know will truly appreciate it? I (Regina) am fully delighted every morning when I can bring tea to my husband in bed. I'm delighted to surprise my housemates by washing the dishes before someone else can get to them. Shinay delights in cooking, especially for others. Just knock on her front door and she'll cook for you! She's delighted by making her husband's lunch each morning before he leaves for work.

Offering delight to others is a unique flavor of love. To feed the hungry, to give drink to the thirsty, to shelter the homeless, to comfort the sorrowful, to relieve suffering wherever it is found – these "Works of Mercy" are the ways in which we can consciously step beyond self-hatred and embrace those in need. Service based in a need to receive thanks won't carry us over the line. Service that is rendered essentially because it is our delight will endure, whether we are thanked or not. But – and this is crucial – remember that the delight will almost always coexist with resistance, difficulty, discomfort, stretching of limits and boundaries, going that extra mile. Delight for us is a life context, not a moment-to-moment experience. Don't you want to be able to look back at your life at the end and say, "I brought delight"?

EXERCISE – *Creating A Delight Menu*

Here are some writing prompts to remind you of your own delights and to encourage you to come up with a few new ones.

Part I: Make lists in response to the following prompts, or simply write about your past experiences and your desires for future play in these domains. Even if you don't have a circle of women-friends, or a partner to share these delights, set yourself a time, place and method for fulfillment.

THE MENU
Foods and eating experiences that delight me. (Not just those that fill your belly, but those that feed your soul too!):

People I love to be around:

Books that have given me delight (or changed my life):

Poetry that moves my soul:

Authors of fiction, non-fiction, poetry whose work inspires me:

Art and creativity forms that have delighted me in the past:

Art forms that bring me great joy now:

Art forms that I have never tried, but would love to play at:

Nearby travel options/destinations that thrill me to think about:

Distance travel options that thrill me to think about:

Sacred places, persons, things that I'd like to visit, meet, engage:

Physical activities that make me smile and appreciate life:

Aspects of the natural world that bring me delight:

Weather conditions that delight me:

Activities with children that would delight both me and them:

Activities with my lover, mother, sister that would delight both of us:

Other delight entrées:

Part II: After you've given some time to the exercise above, write your response to this prompt:
As a result of doing this exercise, I…

Part III: Now, on another piece of paper, write down a promise to yourself (and perhaps to a friend) to actually carry out one of these delights.
What?
When?
Where?
How?
Why?
Solo or with whom?

Then sign and date it. Put it someplace where you will see and read it every day until this delight is fulfilled. Then you get to pick another one off your list!

Remember, this choice for delight is not a one-time kind of thing. We are talking to you about delight as an ongoing relationship. It is meant to be engaged and practiced. In our experience, when we are in relationship with delight, it's pretty impossible to be self-hating.

Inhabit Your Body

Our sister-friend Jewel has taught us lots about living *in* the body. Jewel is a midwife, residing now in Wyoming. During her training she worked for a busy birthing center in El Paso, Texas, just across the border from Ciudad Juarez, Mexico. Here she delivered babies night and day. *Really*, it was a nonstop baby works. What Jewel witnessed during her practice, besides the amazing beauty, stamina and natural love that characterizes women in general (all hail the Goddess!), was how out of touch so many of us are with this precious body instrument. Even though we often identify with the physical form as being all that we are, we women don't love our bodies, and consequently we inflict a huge amount of pain on ourselves, and others, and deny ourselves a huge range of pleasure.

We women don't love our flesh – our fleshiness. Instead, we've been taught to believe that tight skin stretched over bones is glamorous or appealing. Where did we get that idea? What a huge lie it is. Women don't love their womb or their *yonis*. (You can say "vaginas" if you wish, but we prefer the Sanskrit word, which is so much more sacred sounding and doesn't have the same shame attached to it that other words often carry in this culture.) We women don't honor our menstruation, denying that this monthly ritual could be our strongest connection to Earth and raw feminine energy. We're willing to shrink or enlarge our breasts, take medication to do away with monthly periods, fast and exercise extremely and compulsively, or eat and drink compulsively (either end of the spectrum is a demonstration of self-hatred), spend enormous sums on hair and nail treatments to appear beautiful, and basically confine our sex lives either to the bedroom or the fantasy couch of romance-novel sex.

What is your experience?

Jewel Told Us

I started on the midwife path because of a deep trust in the body. I grew up subjected to the same soup of lies, cultural prejudices, and shame around women's bodies as everyone else. The idea that our bodies can't be trusted (*Yikes! we bleed every month! – Cue fear and disgust*) somehow did not take hold of me. (*Thank you, Mom and Dad.*)

What I do as a midwife is nurture and support women in relationship to their changing pregnant bodies. I let them know they are beautiful, that the changes are good and normal, that they don't need to be afraid. Their body is not broken and they can, in fact, trust the body. I loan them my confidence and give them affirmation to be in their body. Then, when the time is ripe, I guard the space in which this amazing instrument, their body, will birth their babe.

It is a simple thing, really. As Ina May Gaskin, a famous midwife, once said, "Your body is not a lemon."

The fact is, as Jewel explains it, that women who know their bodies, appreciate the pleasure of their yonis, honor their unique size and shape and texture, and adorn themselves for the sheer delight of art also have an easier time in birthing their children. And whether we give birth or not, it's important to get to know *all* parts of our selves: the dark, the light, from feet to head, and every crease or round spot in between.

INHABIT THE BODY

To *inhabit our bodies* is the way we like to describe this process of knowing and loving and actually living *in* this body-home of ours. As a yoga teacher, I (Shinay) know that even women who do a lot of sports, who work to keep themselves fit, and even eat super-healthy food are not necessarily *in* their own bodies as they do all this. There is some weird disconnect between the doing and the being. It's almost like they have the body on a leash, walking it, feeding it, pampering it. Like having a pet: something they work with and beautify in order to take out and show off. They're running the body for exercise, but their consciousness is actually outside of that same body, critically observing it and commenting on it all the way. "Oh, good job. Oh yes, you can do it. Oh no, don't stop to eat that." The dialogue goes on and on as the body remains an object to be manipulated, not a tender human woman to be kissed and embraced. They (we) are not *in* the body, *in* the breath, "one with" its sensations, contractions, expansion. Instead, we are still holding ourselves separate, watching and judging the body. This being-sense of full embodiment is actually a profound spiritual practice which brings us out of the total reliance on the rational, analytical mind for our relationships with life. The body is a sorely neglected source of Wisdom.

Our challenge to you, which is the same challenge I (Shinay) make to my yoga students and I (Regina) make to seminar participants, is to first recognize this disconnect in yourself. The mere repetition of *seeing* of it over and over again will, over time, seriously change something. You *can do this*, as I (Shinay) instruct, by simply doing one round of conscious breathing, or one basic stretch, placing full attention to being *inside* the lungs, *inside* the muscles, feeling from the inside out. You will get distracted in the midst of this. Be gentle with yourself. We all have difficulty contacting our own being-presence, in and through the body. Relax and start again. You'll easily recognize in this simple exercise how rarely you are living *here*. That's the practice, and that's the way in which an inner self-cherishing sense is built. That's the way we learn to inhabit the body: by coming home when we recognize and acknowledge that we are away.

Achieving this relationship to being alive and present within the body for a few minutes, or even a few seconds, over and over again is more valuable for self-understanding and self-love than an hour of belabored meditation, or a session of hard and fast motion in which you are "training the dog" – or working the machine. We don't challenge self-hatred by whipping the mind or the physical body into shape. We challenge *never good enough* by being congruent with ourselves – body, mind, emotions, spirit – from the core outward, and in all directions.

This type of awareness, practiced with diligence, will have its effect over time. Imagine being able to stand in the still, silent, strong center of yourself, knowing that you are *here* and knowing that you are *alive* and good. Precious even. The possibilities are limitless. [For more specific instruction in this type of practice, see *Igniting the Inner Life* by Regina Sara Ryan and *Self Observation* by Red Hawk.]

A Thousand Ways

The Beloved knows a thousand ways
to enter your body.

When you were young,
she sent you a lover of flesh
who stood near
to awaken your nature.

Now god is your unseen paramour
arriving without notice
on unexpected occasions.
To discover her,
turn gently, and follow your breath
to the center of your being.
– Dorothy Walters, *Marrow of Flame.*
Used with permission.

Divine Pride

Consider with us a beautiful possibility called "divine pride."
From the tradition of Tibetan Buddhism, in which no concept
of "original sin" characterizes the human condition, Shinay and
I have learned that women are enjoined to honor the intrinsic
nobility and dignity of their female form and all that constitutes
their unique presence in the world: their doubts and failures,
as well as their virtues and successes. The goddess Vajrayogini
clearly declares that every woman is the goddess, and that any
disregard of the human female (by ourselves or by others) is
actually a violation of the divine goddess herself.

Imagine if you had grown up with *that* as your cultural
context! Imagine the awesome power contained in such self-

honoring! Well, as the saying goes, it's never too late to have a happy childhood.

Most women who give birth can naturally bond with their infants, breastfeed with pride and generosity, and give enormous physical affection without holding back. But not all moms know that this same experience of unconditional love they feel for their newborn is a wide-open door for giving the same to themselves. What a clear, unmistakable point of reference we women have to archetypal love and divine pride in the birthing process. Giving birth, a woman knows selflessness in the purest sense of the word. She knows expanded consciousness. She knows both pain and joy beyond measure. She knows beautiful fleshiness and the flow of blood, as well as the sweet aroma of toes and hair and fingers.

Whether we have ever borne a child physically or not, this same celebration of the miracle of birth, and of an infant's inherent beauty, could be extended to ourselves and those around us. Really, as far as we're concerned, this is what Woman (mothers or not) can bring to the world. At the least, most of us probably have a recollection of holding a newborn that, for a moment, lifted us out of self-reference and into the domain of love beyond measure. We can use this as a point of reference for self-honoring. We can return to the body of blessedness.

RETURN HOME: A STOP-GAP EXERCISE

Take a moment to return home – to inhabit this body of yours. Yes, right now! Is there any better time? Bring your attention from your mental center into your solar plexus or abdomen. Keep it there, and keep returning there each time the connection is lost. But do this gently.

Now, observe your breathing. Don't try to deepen it, or change it in any way, just sense how breathing is taking place.

Nude Drawing Class

The instructor turned to the stereo and put on some music as I (Shinay) walked to the stage and took off my robe. I was really doing it! I was getting paid to stand or sit naked for three hours (with short breaks throughout) while a group of art students studied and then drew my figure. I assumed a pose, and relaxed into a mood of meditation.

After the first twenty-minute session, I walked around the room and asked the artists to see their pictures. Some drew, a few painted, one worked with charcoal, one ballpoint, another pen and ink. I was amazed. What I saw on the paper was not my narrow-minded twenty-six-year-old critical opinion of my naked body. What I saw before me was an array of color, texture, and vibrancy, captured in all levels of detail. I was no longer solid but malleable. Object yes, objectified no – like the Latin word *objectum*,"a thing presented to the mind." I was presented, and their artistic minds and hearts created.

I consider myself a pretty body-positive person, but what I experienced after looking at their images was something far more interesting than the limited sense I had of my own body. What I experienced was a sense of liberation. The student artists gave me permission to be inspired by my physical form in a whole new way: wrinkles became interesting features to look at, fat transformed into the depth the picture needed, and bones changed into lines that captured the eye. This experience brought me back into my body such that I was living from the inside, not judging from the outside. I had more confidence, a richer/deeper perspective of what's beautiful, and a rekindled love for my own human form because it had been instrumental in creating extraordinary art.

Stay with this for a half-minute or so. Keep returning home each time the connection is lost. Soften. Gently.

Next, sense the dimensions of your physical body and how it is currently located in space. Where are your feet in relationship to your head? Where is your right hand in relationship to your left hand? Notice any differences in sensation in any part of the body. Notice the external body sensations. Note the internal body sensations: levels of tightness or tension, of heat or cold. Sense your whole body. Stay with this step and keep returning to it for thirty seconds or so.

Now, relax your whole body. Relax more deeply. Stay here. Begin again.

> *The destination is the present. It must be constantly renewed with every breath or the connection is lost.*
>
> — Red Hawk

Self-Massage

So often when I (Shinay) bump into something, cut my finger while chopping veggies, or stub my toe, it's an indicator that I'm out of touch with myself, and an invitation to "return home." One practice that has been *extremely* useful for me is self-massage. I do it daily. Self-massage helps me know the boundaries of my own physical body. It quite literally puts me back *into* my body. Sometimes I do it two or three times a day. I hop in a hot shower so my skin is warm, then I gently towel dry off and apply sesame oil all over my skin – from my feet to my ears. Oil in the Ayurveda system equals love. I've found this practice nourishing and rejuvenating. It's also very calming to the nervous system.

For those who are a bit reticent, I suggest starting with a one-minute foot rub. Or take one minute to give yourself a "body hug." Squeeze your arms, your shoulders, your neck; run your fingers through your hair; move down and massage your breasts, your belly, your buttocks, your thighs, making loving circles around your knees; rub your calves and shins, ankles and feet. The word in Japanese for healing is *te-ate*; it literally means *to apply hands*.

Do this practice of self-massage with loving-kindness. Hating ourselves for the way we look does not serve. Judging our bodies and limiting ourselves with shoulds, coulds, and if onlys is unproductive.

LIFE AS GODDESS

What we're pointing to here with regard to living *in and as* the body is a deep descent into sacred territory. Such work-on-self (accepting and loving our physicality; using it as a doorway to compassion, the Great Love) has genuine implications for all humanity. As we engage this intention to embrace Woman, the Objective Feminine, in and as ourselves, we stake a claim that may be our only hope to save the world! Aggression, denial, separation, power…these modes of human interaction aren't increasing genuine happiness anywhere. The qualities that characterize the Goddess, the Great Mother – whether she is Mary of Nazareth or Kali of Calcutta – are fierce without violence; are open-eyed, inclusive, honoring of life in all its many forms. Connecting ourselves with the body of Goddess is a way to build divine pride and motivation for action (if only the action of unqualified self-acceptance). The Goddess embodies life. She teaches us sacred physicality. She encourages us to move beyond the self-limiting mindsets and old forms of silly selfishness that keep us isolated from ourselves and others.

The difference between a woman who is disenfranchised from herself and one who loves and honors herself may hinge on appreciation of the sacred body. When the larger context of relationship with the Goddess is held to, an individual woman ceases to be the focus of her own life. She isn't aiming at a perfect physique. She isn't celebrating a wrinkle-free face. Instead, the deep desire to inhabit and express the essence of Woman in a world that is so sorely in need of the Feminine takes the front seat. When that happens, a new view toward personal problems and a new dedication to the whole, to others, can naturally arise.

For a fantastical example, imagine that you suddenly got a letter informing you that you had been found out – that the lineage of your parents and grandparents had been fabricated to keep you safe, whereas in reality you were the protected offspring of royalty, and that you were next in line to be the reigning queen of a small country which honored its monarchs with great respect. Knowing all this, you might hold your body differently, yes? You might start to walk with greater dignity. You might find yourself planning how to use the huge wealth at your disposal for what *really* needs serving among your newly inherited people. As queen, you'd have these many possibilities.

It's a crazy thought, certainly, but it serves to make our point that when we can identify with the awesome dignity and abundant generosity of the Feminine, our own small problems are subsumed, at least temporarily. We suddenly find that the world is different. In this example we didn't have to "do" anything or "look like" anything to "be" that queen. She was already within us, simply awaiting recognition in order to show her benevolent hand.

This understanding is the real basis for practices that involve the Goddess, or the Divine Mother, which many traditions advocate. Within Catholicism, some fortunate ones among us were told, "Your body is the Blessed Virgin Mary." The traditions of Goddess-worship in India will tell us the same thing – that we *are* that Goddess, never separate. When a woman is reminded that her body is a temple, a sacred artifact, a vessel...she sits up straighter. She graciously attends to those around her who need loving care. It's not just rhetoric. It's a secret, too long well kept, that has the possibility of changing our orientation to life and to our own bodies.

Our friend and sister Aditi Devi (who writes books about the great Hindu goddesses) has instructed us that the uterus /vagina/cervix of the woman's body is a powerhouse of communication, but this channel is turned off most of the time. Fear and ignorance and self-shame are the turn-off factors. As a countermeasure, she invites us to place our gentle attention there throughout the day, to learn how the energy moves here – swirling, clenching, bubbling, settling. She invites us to listen to our yoni (the female genitals). She invites us to invoke the Divine Feminine to bless us in our desire to make this area of the body a sacred chamber – for pleasure, for prayer, for warning and preparing us, for communication. Especially for letting us know "yes" and "no."

Imagine having so much self-love and self-appreciation that we could stay attuned to the energetic center located in the yoni. It is something to consider. It is something to talk about with your women-friends. Now *that* would be getting beyond the *blah, blah, blah* rather quickly, yes?

Making a distinction between "feminism" and "the Feminine" and between "woman" and "Woman" presents a lovely challenge that inspires lots of insight and questions – for us and apparently for others. Remember that the Feminine is an energetic life force that is present (at least in seed form) in all of us, regardless of gender. Realize that the Feminine principle is that aspect or pole of creation that "births" life from within itself and in others, nurtures and feeds that life, educates it, touches and caresses it in all its many forms, forgives and blesses and eases it, holding its hands as sickness, old age and death approach. The responsibility, privilege, and joy to reveal and act upon this Feminine Principle is for everyone – men as well as women.

How might your life have been different, if, deep within, you carried an image of the Great Mother, and, when things seemed very, very bad, you could imagine that you were sitting in the lap of the Goddess,
> held tightly...
> embraced, at last.
And, that you could hear Her saying to you,
> "I love you...
> I love you and I <u>need</u> you to bring
> forth your self."
And, if, in that image, you could see the Great Mother looking to Her daughters, looking to each woman to reveal, in her own life, the beauty, strength, and wisdom of the Mother.

How might your life be different?

– Judith Duerk, Circle of Stones,
Woman's Journey to Herself

A LINEAGE OF MA

Many of us witnessed self-hatred in our moms, or grandmas, or aunties. They didn't mean to teach this, but they were so soaked in it we couldn't help but be affected. The unconditional love that mother knows for her newborn got quickly contaminated by mother's pain and fear. (Our own ability to receive and rest in unconditional love was similarly wounded.) Without help, our moms stumbled along, just doing the best they could. Some of them admirably. Some, not so, as their pain was simply too great. Lord have mercy on our mothers!

I (Regina) love to share the story of having found a loving mother as a role model and support. In the summer of 1988, I met a woman in Freiburg, Germany, named Dina Rees. Dina was a being of dazzling love and good-humored service. She had been a medical doctor. She had ten adopted children. She was a poet and writer. She was a pilgrim on the spiritual path who traveled throughout India, healing and learning. She was honored in her own country as well as in India as a living witness and embodiment of Ma, the Divine Mother.

Dina's teaching was simple. Everyone must be Mother… to themselves, to everyone else, and especially to all the world's children. Everyone must care for the Earth, must be attuned to the ways he or she can relieve suffering, through forgiveness and gentleness. Everyone must respect the life he or she carries in the body, giving themselves and others the space and support needed for their creativity (which is also their love) to "come to full term" by courageously enduring its labor pains so it might be born into an environment of conscious friends and family who will continue to raise it, encouraging every step.

During this remarkable meeting, I remember that for a split second the elder's face shifted and took on a most profound familiarity. Looking at Dina, I was shocked to recognize *my*

Dina Rees

own face. The teaching was clear: we were one. The enormous love that I felt being radiated from Dina was actually my own love reflected back to me.

From that moment, I "took" Dina as my mother, my tangent point to unconditional love and acceptance. For me, it didn't matter that I had only spent three hours in her presence. What had been awakened in me was true mother compassion within myself, and compassion for the world at large.

Back home, I enlarged the photo I had taken of Dina and hung it on the wall of my room. I thought about my beloved "mother" almost every day. And even though Dina died a few years later, I continued to "go to her" for advice, and prayed to her. Some mornings, as I drank a cup of tea, I would sit with Dina, alive in her own heart, and let myself be expanded into the love that was not separate from either of us.

There are great human mothers everywhere who await the arrival of their daughters. They will not be perfect icons. They

Wisdom from Betty Jo, age 91

Betty: "The ravages of age are taking hold, and I sometimes ask myself should I do something about it? Should I get those injections in my face? And then I just get over it! Sure the media says I should do this or that, and anti-aging is a big seller. But, I'm beyond anti-aging."

Both women laugh.

"So what works for living life to the fullest?" asks Shinay, still laughing.

"Laughter helps! And you just say 'phooey' on all that other hype, 'I'm just going to live my life.'"

Shinay: "Because aging is a natural process, right?"

"Yes," says Betty, "and at ninety you're not going to look like you did when you were twenty. I'm not into self-flagellation. There are a lot of good things about getting old, and a lot of it is sloughing off what used to bother me. It's a good time of life. Read more books that will help you let go, and have courage to jump into your life and move towards something that you love. Don't get addicted, to anything, particularly to things staying the same. It's not necessary to listen to all this anti-aging stuff. Surround yourself with people who love you, who care, and people whom you love; people who nurture your well-being. Just let the rest go!"

will have plenty of wrinkles. Yet, a woman with a heart of gold is not as hard to find as you might initially expect. Ask around. Ask your group. "Who are your mothers?" would be a great question to consider in your circle, or simply with one other friend. Together you might be able to assign yourselves a new lineage of Ma's. As I love to tell women, "It's never too late to be nurtured by the unconditional love of Mother."

Mother is the body of God. Mother is the body of creation! "Being Mother" awaits us as we learn to inhabit the body. By being Mother, in the largest sense of that term, we can irradiate the parasites of self-hatred that hover everywhere. *She* will be triumphant!

EXERCISE – *Ideas to Contemplate and Write About*

1. There are women suffering everywhere. Women who will not show up in bathing suits, or at the gym, or at some festival on the town square. Women whose bodies have been scarred by fire, or torture, or illness. Women struggling to accept a broken body that can't be fixed. You've seen them, here or there, haven't you? What has been your reaction? What is your reflection of that experience now? Write about this. Or share your reflections with a friend. What might you offer such a woman if she were your sister?

2. The perfect-body myth. Even though you don't believe it, you are still influenced by it. Tell the truth about how.

3. Everything fades. Consider interviewing a very old (80 years or above) woman and talking about this subject of inhabiting the body. Or, have such a conversation with a Hospice nurse or friend who has recently attended a dying female relative. Discuss your findings. Write a story or poem.

Decidedly, these are difficult subjects. We offer them because open-eyed bravery is necessary in challenging the lie of *never good enough*. Courage!

Write Your Way Home

For almost two weeks, I (Regina) awaited his letter. Not some legal document or business contract, but a reply from a mentor whom I had written to for advice. Older than I, this man is also a poet, and one I admire greatly for his deep dedication to the path of the heart. When the envelope finally arrived, it was stuffed. A short two pages that basically confirmed my own inner sense of things in the questions I had asked him, and five poems, each on a separate sheet of paper and each relating to the struggle I had expressed in writing to him in the first place. What a happy day it was!

This letter in hand, I then had another beautiful (and tangible) memento of our love and mutual dedication to the work of self-knowledge, self-remembrance. I also had a small series of meditation topics (the poems), each affirming an essential truth that easily gets obscured when the lie of *never good enough* kicks in for me.

I don't save every bit of mail I receive, certainly. But I do save all his letters. I also save significant missives from other correspondents who write to me expressing their love, their support, their insight into the subjects that most matter to us. These letters contain an energetic connection to my friends and mentors. Simply holding them on a bad day somehow gives me courage. I am reminded of my love for writers and their love for me. I am reminded of what is true.

RADICAL WRITING

We are not Luddites! Shinay and I still use e-mail and several forms of social media. We each host a website for our work, and Shinay keeps a vibrant blog. *And*, we are happy and proud to confess that we are part of a small radical fringe: we still write letters with pen and ink on paper or send cards with small notes within. We use postage stamps (how quaint!) to get our most personal and meaningful communications from one part of the country, even the world, to another. We write because handwritten (even computer-printed) personal letters received through the mail (or left on the doorstep) cause delight to us when we receive them, and we're determined to bring delight to others as well by writing to them.

Writing a personal letter about what matters most is a way we can articulate for ourselves, with the blessed witness of another, what we know to be true but may be forgetting. We use our letters as we use journaling, to explore the questions that gnaw at our ankles, to express as simply but as graciously as possible how our love is playing out in the present, or the ways in which love seems obscured. We write to a friend, a mentor, or a sister because we want to be connected beyond the *blah blah blah*. And you and we all know that a lot of electronic communication is filled with these blahs. We write as a way to contribute to others, putting someone else on the radar of our attention, rather than forever obsessing through self-scrutiny.

We know this is a big invitation, a Radical Move to suggest that you do some writing – through a letter or a journal entry, through a poem or story! We're making the request anyway.

After all, we accept that you are asking us for realistic ways and means to deflate the lie of *never good enough*. Writing from the inside out is one of those ways.

"BUT I CAN'T WRITE"

Okay, we've heard this before, *ad nauseum*, in fact. The old Inner Critic at work here; the old Blank-Page-Paralysis Syndrome. While for some of us writing is a passion that can't be delayed, for many others it's held as a type of self-torture. You are not alone if the "I hate to write" or "I can't write" program is playing in your head as you read about actually writing something, anything, even a brief letter. We are glad that some of you have brought it up; glad that we can address this fear or reticence about writing straight away. Even if you love to write, read on, as you undoubtedly have other areas in your own life where the old program of resistance and self-doubt is keeping you stuck. Looking at our dismissal strategies for why we "can't" or "won't" or simply "don't like to" play with any new venture is actually a dynamic clue in resolving the whole dilemma of *never good enough*.

But before we share that secret, listen to this: if you finally *choose* to never write a letter, or learn to tango, or climb that mountain you can see in the distance – or actually *do* anything else that comes to mind in considering this Radical Move – be assured that you are still lovely and good, and important to us. So relax. Please simply read this section anyway for the principles of working with self-hatred that it contains, and consider these principles with your friend or group. Shinay and I are quite ecstatic about this Radical Move, but we do appreciate that not everyone shares our views about writing or risk taking or starting to learn a new skill. The important thing is to *choose* whatever you do, or don't do, as a grown-up, not to simply react with the same old childish defaults (about this or anything else) that keep life boring, *blah*. This Radical Move is our nudge. Take it or not, but lighten up about it either way.

And the secret? Well, as writers and teachers, we know Madame Inner Critic intimately. She keeps me (Regina) out of bookstores (and sometimes out of libraries) because all the new publications on the shelves are "so much better written" than whatever I'm currently working on. Shinay's Madame Inner Critic comes up with awesomely lame excuses for not writing. When she picks up her journal to write, her Madame reminds her that her handwriting isn't pretty enough; that she's a terrible speller; and that if she can't finish the first draft of a poem and do it perfectly, she'd better not even try.

This critic lady never quits! As writers, we've simply learned to give her a kiss and thank her for urging us to do our best. We thank her for reminding us of the truth that someone else will always do "it" better, according to somebody else's standard – and we let her know that this will not keep us from our task, regardless of how insistent she becomes. We give her a nod, reach out to embrace her, and then step forward.

> *Knowing we have done our best and it simply*
> *wasn't enough opens our hearts to other human*
> *beings whose best has likewise failed.*
> **– Marion Woodman,** *Dancing in the Flames*

We *know* that Madame Inner Critic in this domain of writing is a twin sister to Lady Self-Hatred, or Queen Never-Good-Enough. We know that writing "beyond" her, around her, and even *with* her tucked under our arm (rather than allowing her the CEO's chair) is a serious derailment of the train of excuses that keeps us comparing, devaluing, procrastinating, or apologizing – about writing or anything. (We know women who are great cooks but will apologize in advance for the meal, or deflect any thanks for their contribution to our lives, or even deny their skills by telling us that so-and-so is a *real* cook, while they are only hacks.) Your decision to write a letter to (or cook a meal for) a friend or loved one, or even a perfect stranger, is a symbolic declaration of your willingness to risk. It is a declaration that the Pulitzer Prize (or a Michelin star) is not your goal, but rather that care and delight (C.D.) are the degrees you really want on your resume.

Like us, you've probably received letters or cards containing personal notes that were difficult to read because of the correspondent's handwriting, his or her lack of mastery of the English language, or their spelling and punctuation. Still, through it all, you've probably still felt their heart, their questions, their tears, and their reaching out. We don't want you to write because you're good at it. We want you to write because we know you are committed to Woman, and Woman touches others.

In writing for yourself alone, as long as you feel no obligation to show it, you can attempt to put your heart's desire into a few sentences, your questions into a few paragraphs, your gratitude into a page, or even two. This is valuable practice in the art of self-understanding and self-appreciation. Are you willing to risk doing the same for another? To kiss Lady Critic and move on anyway?

Write a letter.

Start with a Disclaimer
"I don't have the words to tell you how much you mean to me…"

"If I could communicate from my heart to yours, without words, you'd know a secret that I'm afraid to speak…"

"It is hard for me to put on paper what is working on me (working me over!) these days..."

As your coaches in the process of working this book, Shinay and I are not advocates of apology and excuses, which are generally ways in which we disempower the truth of our love, basic goodness, and awesome intentions. However, as writers, we know a little trick that might prove helpful to you in starting on this (or any) Radical Move. Simply put, we can gain a lot of momentum to further our writing, or to advance any new venture we are considering, by beginning with a generic disclaimer (writers seem to need this), or just plain admitting *what we don't know*. In her much-loved poem "The Summer Day," the poet Mary Oliver got a lot of mileage from her disclaimer that she did not know what prayer was. Instead, in this piece she reflected upon the delight of feeling "blessed" as she roamed the fields watching grasshoppers and other interesting critters. While she's declared that she may not know about prayer, she makes a sterling case for the power of paying attention. Her whole poem invites her reader to be present to life, just as it is!

This method of disclaiming of what we don't know is one of my (Regina's) most frequent instructions to my writing students. Write what you don't know, what you are not sure of, what is being questioned, what is still a mystery, I advise them. The more you can distinguish what you don't know about love, or God, or friendship, or self-hatred, the more you clear the ground for some small certainty to bud. So you might write, "I do not know how or where I first adopted the belief that I wasn't good enough, but I do know that this lie isn't useful to a life of joy." Or, "I don't know for sure that 'not good enough' is a lie; maybe I really am 'not good enough' according to someone else's standard, but I do know that I am not alone in this assessment of self – that women everywhere make this judgment, and that it robs us of power and joy!"

Do you see how declaring what you *don't know* or *don't understand* can be a jumping off place for considering what you *do know*, what you *do understand*, or simply what *you decide* to call it?

I Don't Know

Oh God, I do not know how to pray.
And because I don't, I have to offer only
what I'm sure of,
what I can do,
and call that prayer.

So, let this breath be the prayer.
Let this distraction be the prayer.
Let this drinking a cup of tea be the prayer.
Let missing someone be the prayer.
Let the vastness of the night sky be the prayer...

Oh God, in my helplessness,
from nowhere, with nothing
let these poor prayers, like flowers
draw You to the garden
from which their fragrance arises.
Amen

– from "Prayer of Not Knowing," Regina

Shinay clearly remembers starting on a writing project before her first trip to India. The issues I suggested she address included: What I don't know about India. What I don't want to experience in India. What I probably won't like about traveling with other people. What I don't expect to encounter. And then even more raw challenges, like: What I don't want to see in myself. What might send me running for home. What I won't accept about my companions on this trip.

About this assignment, Shinay wrote:

> Not trying to "know" or claim to know anything, I was "off the hook," and felt free to explore for myself what I did know. Without the "should" of knowing, I had an opportunity to *not* be perfect, to *not* have all the answers, to be in quest of something greater in my writing and in myself. This is a powerful space to live in, this space of honesty and clarity about "I don't know."

We suggest that you try this disclaimer method whenever you're stuck for what to write or what to say. Use it to kickstart the letter to a friend that may be the beginning of a radical lifestyle of putting relationship and delight above the need for certainty and the assurance of perfection at every step. Remember, anything worth doing is worth doing imperfectly!

MINING FOR GOLD

The Radical Move of writing a letter may be the first step in keeping a journal, writing a story, an article, or even a book, either alone or with the help of your friend or sister. Our passion for this Move comes out of the need to find clarity within, to express our love and creativity in form, and to pass on to others what is being learned or discovered. While your primary way of standing up for self-appreciation may be painting or dancing or cooking beautiful food, communicating it through language is an invaluable adjunct for yourself and others. We are deeply inspired by the memoirs (or even short reflections) of artists from all genres – explorers, healers, athletes, disabled men and women – who have mined their work, distilled it, and presented it for public scrutiny within the medium of language.

Until you write something down, you may not actually *know* how much you know (or don't know) about it. The writer C. S. Lewis said that we write in order to discover what we know. From this perspective, writing is a type of gold mining. To start writing is to enter that deep mine of yourself. The process of writing/mining will convince you that wisdom-ore exists in you, and can be reached, tapped, brought to the surface and used for healing, for re-enlivening, for creative expression.

In our experience, we can't *fully* digest what we're getting from life until we try to articulate it for ourselves or others, and putting it down on paper is a form of articulation. Try it. If you simply write down what's been happening for you, especially in the domain of heart and soul, you'll find that you begin to "own" it at a whole new level. Without writing them down, our insights are just threads floating around in the air... in our hair...somewhere! If we catch hold of these threads and start aiming them through the eye of a "needle" (writing instrument; that's what articulating thoughts through writing does), we can use that thread to make something that will last. Maybe even something we can start to "wear."

We've all got the makings of a really beautiful garment, and right at hand; but many of us aren't creating it.

WRITE WITH A FRIEND

If you have a single companion or a circle of women to work with, even a short writing exercise each time you gather is a useful way to deepen your intimacy with each other. Writing with a friend is a brilliant way to inspire your solitary writing at other times, particularly in the days prior to your get-togethers.

For years, Shinay and I met for a writing mentorship. Besides our study of great works, we simply wrote together. I might suggest an obvious topic based on something that was currently up for me, like, "The most challenging roadblock in my spiritual path at this time is..." Or she might suggest an even more serious topic, like "Carrots and their role in my life..." And then we would spend only ten to fifteen minutes writing, quickly, so that our Madame Editor-Critic didn't get the upper hand every time.

But "quick writing" didn't mean sloppy stream-of-consciousness drivel! There's enough of that around on Internet blogs these days. No, our words were to be chosen with careful consideration aiming at raw honesty. We forbade ourselves and one another to write about stuff we'd merely *heard about* but hadn't lived through, unless we specifically owned up to that. We tabooed something we'd only casually thought about but hadn't felt with accompanying sensations – something we "wanted," but weren't yet willing to bleed for. This was no easy task.

The list of topics we were inspired to write about was limitless. No such thing as "writer's block" when the chair you are sitting on could become the subject for a "quick write." The mood of open-eyed realness that easily emerged from honest writing about even chairs or carrots was often positively delicious. This is the type of writing we recommend to you with your friend or group, or at least with yourself.

Writing a letter to a friend, or an attentive "quick write" with a companion, is still bound to be tainted by the lie we're stalking in this book. Still, we do the writing anyway, because we're more interested in self-knowledge than in self-recrimination. More interested in caring and love than in perfection. Writing practice is one way to switch from defense to inquiry, from blame to curiosity, as the celebrated essayist Philip Lopate reminds us, in his book, *To Show and To Tell*:

> And here we come to one of the main stumbling blocks placed before effective personal writing: self-hatred.
>
> It is an observable fact that most people don't like themselves, in spite of being decent-enough human beings – certainly not war criminals – in spite of the many self-help books urging us to befriend and think positively about ourselves. Why this self-dislike should be so prevalent I cannot pretend to understand; all I can say, from my vantage point as a teacher and anthologist of the personal essay, is that an odor of self-disgust mars many performances in this genre and keeps many would-be personal writers from developing into full-fledged professionals. They exhibit a form of stuttering, of never being able to get past the initial, superficial self-presentation and delving into the wreck of personality with gusto.
>
> The proper alternative to self-dislike is not being pleased with oneself – a smug complacency that comes across as equally distasteful – but being *curious* about oneself. Such self-curiosity...can only grow out of...detachment or distance from

oneself...I am convinced that self-amusement is a discipline that can be learned; it can be practiced even by people such as myself, who have at times a strong self-mistrust.

This Radical Move is about using writing to express *curiosity* about yourself, without judgment; to be objective, interested, even grateful that your own quirks and failings (and not-knowings) are going to provide you with so much great material. As an added bonus, what you will reveal to yourself is likely to serve somebody else. We promise you this! Both of us are continually gratified and surprised to learn that admitting our failings, our imagined "sins," is one sure way of building intimacy and relationship. Amazingly, sometimes the nastier or darker your revelation is, the more it will serve someone who is going through the same darkness. Your Lady Nasty seriously wants to have dinner with you. She has a lot to teach you. In our experience, too much "spiritual insight" without self-expression and action will give us indigestion and constipation. We know that writing is a way to digest and circulate and eliminate.

WRITING YOUR WAY HOME

Most of us are great at giving advice to others, at least in our heads! If only the other – she or he – would ask and listen to us, we know *exactly* what to tell them to do (or not do) to turn their life around. Inside ourselves, as they ramble on, we may be thinking, "Just quit your whining, bitch," or "That guy is a total asshole and you know it. Get him out of your life, will you?" or "Your body is luscious, if only you would *lush it*. Forget that crap about needing to have firm thighs," and so on.

Most of our friends probably don't want to hear such opinions about their lives. But *if* they sincerely ask, it would be a real contribution if you had honed your honesty skills enough that you could speak what you see while letting them know that you love them regardless of whether they took your advice or not. After all, your opinions are generated not essentially because you want to control your friends (Or do you? Please tell the truth about that), but because you really want to relieve their suffering. We honor you for this.

If you are able to tell the truth to yourself about what *others* can or should do, are you willing to tell the same truth about what *you* can or should do? If not, why not? If so, what are you waiting for? Explore this series of questions in your own writing, and use what you've written to spark discussion with your sisters and friends.

From Shinay's Journal

I'm sitting on my couch, it's Sunday afternoon, and I'm crying (wailing actually) because I just hosted a family brunch: made delicious food, and then it all went to shit. Half the food wound up in the trash. Really, I had gone out of my way to make something for everyone (first mistake?).

I'm blaming them now, and replaying all their side comments, overlaying my interpretations on what happened. I am on that slippery slope and moving fast on the downward spiral toward self-hatred.

I don't want to call my sister and ask why she and her kids threw their food away, and why they were so tense. I'm afraid she wouldn't be honest with me. I'm afraid too because I don't want to cause more waves (I know how she hates confrontation), especially as this just might be all my projection. I imagine already what my sister will say.

(Long self-pitying pause)

And yet...maybe it isn't all about me. Maybe *they* were just going through their own stuff. And maybe they simply *didn't* like my food and they just wanted to eat fried eggs instead. Isn't that okay? Well, yeah... Maybe they felt obligated to come over in the first place.

I am not going to just ask her. I'm going to work with this myself. I want to know, for myself, that no matter what the cause (actually, maybe my food did suck. It was a little dry...), it doesn't mean I have to buy the lie of "Not Enough." In some people's eyes, I will never be enough, and *that* is okay.

Later...

What happened during Sunday brunch was totally personal and totally impersonal. I had/have every right to feel hurt. Grieve even, for good food that wound up in the trash. And everyone else had every right to throw their food away.

GIFT is given without strings attached (expectations, desires, ulterior motives, personal agendas). I had an expectation.

ENOUGH is about

Intellect – reassurance.

Body – breathing.

Heart – softening.

Even though it hurts

Spirit/Soul – given permission to expand.

This current Radical Move is a gift we bequeath to you as a means to "come home" – to *discover who you are*, and to examine "failings" as phenomena to observe rather than sins to atone for. Get curious. Get honest. Get out of the way. See that you are human and that self-doubt is what humans in this cultural milieu are programmed to do. But avoid blaming anybody else for this, as much as you can – and don't blame yourself.

> *Let us remember...that in the end we go to poetry*
> *[or prose or art of any kind] for one reason, so*
> *that we might more fully inhabit*
> *our lives and the world in which we live them,*
> *and*
> *that if we more fully inhabit these things, we*
> *might*
> *be less apt to destroy both.*
>
> **– Christian Winman**
> **editor, www.PoetryMagazine.org**

GUIDELINES

Here are a few guidelines to use if you wish to engage in this writing process, whether writing a letter or writing with a friend.

1. Keep the writing sessions or the letters short, at least in the beginning. Unless you are curious about writing, don't burden yourself with hours or days of empty writing time. We find that one or two ten-minute writing sessions can generate a letter filled with enormous creativity, or reveal a series of curious sentences that can be further developed. After you're warmed up, you may want to order a second cup of coffee or tea and continue with what you've started. I (Regina) generally write my letters in segments: *Monday morning, 6 AM, a few opening paragraphs. Let the letter sit for a day or two. Continue on Wednesday at tea in the café, write for half*

an hour. Conclude the letter on Saturday afternoon, with a glass of wine in front of the fireplace.

2. Give yourself no grief over what you're *not* doing. Celebrate what you *are* doing. Even one ten-minute session a week, or a day (even better), is better than not writing at all and feeling guilty or judging yourself poorly. Get it?

3. Always read back slowly and respectfully what you've written, and tell Madame Editor-Critic to go use the restroom as you do. If you are alone, read silently to yourself. If you are with one or more friends, read out loud. No apologies before, during, or after. Get that? *No apologies,* such as "This isn't very good but…" or "I didn't really get rolling on this one…" or "Oh, yours was so good; well, here's mine…" – whatever. Recognize how easily you fall into the "No" habit. Forget that! It's not only a lie, but it is very, very, very boring. (You know it, as you too probably get totally bored when others won't get off this track!) Life is too short to be "No"-ing around endlessly. Instead, honor your words. Treat them as sacred symbols. And give yourself permission to enjoy the simple art of communication. Take a friendly attitude toward your thoughts, your words, your self.

4. Keep your letters to be answered, your stationary, and your favorite pen in a folder or case dedicated solely to that purpose. Keep your free-writing in a notebook saved particularly for writing practice and journal keeping. No paper napkins or the backs of shopping lists. Whether you use conventional pen and paper – which I (Regina) highly recommend – or whether you use your laptop or desktop is up to you. Please don't use your phone. It's too small, too easy, and too rushed!

Write. Write. Write. And keep in mind that any digital writing can be superficial because it can be so fast, so wherever you write use attention and care. Let each word be a sacred trust. No lies. No complaints. No apologies. No pretensions.

5. Befriend Madame Critic, and honor that she will not ever go away. But she can become a sister, and an honored guest at your table, rather than somebody to shame you, blame you, or demand that you stop because your writing is just not good enough. You are not writing to please your Critic, you are writing to please...well...that's a good question. Who are you writing for?

EAVESDROPPING ON A WRITING CLASS

"Put only today's date at the top of a clean sheet of paper," the writing coach instructed. She was smiling broadly, apparently having a great time in sharing what she most loved.

"Feel the emotions that arise for you when you look at this empty space. Be brave. You won't fall off the edge, I promise. But I know it can be scary to begin, with all the programs in your head saying, 'I'm not a good writer,' or 'What can I write about?'"

"You read my mind?" laughed Amethyst, an older student, and a few others in the group giggled nervously.

"It's only necessary to start with one honest sentence," the mentor told them, making Ernest Hemingway's description of writing her own. "You can do that much, no? Anybody can. One simple, honest, declarative sentence? Nothing fancy. In fact, the stuff of your ordinary mind is much more profound that you are willing to admit. But you have to get it out on paper first, before you can know that." She was riffing off instruction from the great Tibetan Buddhist master, Chögyam

Trungpa, who had been a teacher of the poet Allan Ginsberg for years. They used to swap poetry. "Ordinary mind contains eternal perceptions," wrote Trungpa, and Ginsberg shared that forever with the participants in his writing workshops.

"Let's each write one honest sentence about an incident that challenged us this week, okay?" She wasted no time in getting them to the task. "Go."

After less than three minutes she said, "Stop. Put your pen down and read slowly what you've written to yourself." She paused. "Listen to the voice of the self-hater giving you feedback as you survey your work."

"I like what I wrote," exclaimed Ruby, one of the younger women in the class. "I really like it."

"Great," she replied. "A critic is sometimes positive, often negative. But either way we're not going to stop, either to beat ourselves up or to take a bow. We're writing. That's it. What we like or don't like doesn't matter. What we think or feel makes no difference. We're writing to understand ourselves and what we know, not to get published."

The room took a collective deep breath. The students/ friends were relaxing.

"Okay, now write the next true sentence that follows from the sentence you just wrote. And remember, this is not about gorgeous word craft; essentially it is about touching your own truth and threading the needle with that. I'll give you a full ten minutes. Write one sentence after another, as many as you have time for. Just keep telling the truth."

"What if I write something that doesn't feel like the truest truth?" asked Jade, a perfectionist if ever there was one.

"Easy," the coach said, "start your next sentence by writing, 'What I really meant to say was…' and go on from there." Jade smiled.

The group went to work. Here's some of what they wrote:

~ "When I'm with my mother, who has cancer, I don't know how to hide; I don't know how to tell a joke; I don't know if I should simply shut up or keep chatting."

~ "Being with my teenage daughter is like drinking chilled vodka martinis during Mass."

~ "My self-hater's voice still rattled on during meditation practice today. But I heard it like a toad's croak in an otherwise quiet pond."

~ "I'm so pissed off I could scream, but who can I scream at? I want it over, I want no more pain for those I love. How interesting."

~ "Everything changes, and so quickly. Today, Mom asked me to rub her feet and she has never asked to be touched before. I think this is a big indicator that we're getting to trust each other."

~ "I'm jealous. But, what I really mean to say is that I'm glad my daughter has a friend she can rely on, and I want one too. I want her to be loved and to feel trust with somebody. That's most important to me."

As they read to each other, she encouraged all to be brave and spacious. She knew it was hard to be vulnerable. She poured more iced tea all around. Reading their work aloud was not nearly as difficult as many of the group had imagined. Feeling closer to each other made up for any possible comparisons.

EXERCISE – *Topics or Questions to Explore in Free-writing or Letters*

Gift yourself with a quick 10-minute writing session on one or more of the topics below (1 – 8), followed by a quick response to 9. Thank you.

1. What I know about self-hatred is…

2. What I don't know about self-hatred is…

3. I easily fall into self-doubt, hatred, negativity when…

4. What (or who) temporarily relieves, waylays, or distracts me from self-hatred and self-doubt is…

5. If I were to face self-hatred squarely, without turning away, I might…

6. Who do I know who seems to be beyond or above self-hatred?

How are they *being* that gives me this indication?

Write a quick portrait of him or her.

7. When self-hatred arises in my mind, my body responds by…

8. If I focus essentially on my bodily responses and my breath, what if anything happens to self-hatred thinking?

9. **Final topic:** Read back over what you've written on any of these exercises and then respond:

As a result of doing this writing exercise, I…

Start a Secret Blessing Club

"I bless you, I bless you, I bless you," I (Regina) announced to my friends one day. Some looked embarrassed. Others were obviously perplexed. A few had wrinkled brows that said, in effect, "Ah, there she goes again."

"Would it make any difference if I said, I thank you; I remember you; I see who you are; I'm so grateful that you're in my life?" I asked. A few warming smiles followed.

The connection between self-hatred and gratitude, or rather the lack of gratitude, is clear. We all know how certain skewed remembrances of ourselves get stuck and predominate in our consciousness. These mistake-memories or "less than" images shadow the sun that could be touching us. They obscure what *is* working, what is tenderly growing, what is potential. Even as we may be craving love and affection from others, we are often categorically unwilling to give it unconditionally to ourselves, still holding onto the "undeserving" lie. We simply aren't trained in seeing, or acknowledging, the good.

Shinay and I see the same hard and cold tendencies in our friends. They have minimal gratitude for the efforts they have made, but plenty of discouragement about those they haven't. At best, we could say that we all suffer from a type of stinginess

– we forget or overlook the need to practice gratitude to life, or God, for the miracles that surround us, and instead reinforce lots of fear and victimization about what isn't secured. Many of us can barely tolerate hearing from our closest friends that we actually have the "right stuff" – *any* right stuff: from intelligence, to looks, to kindness, to generosity. Instead, we consistently turn aside compliments, in effect spitting in the face of a benefactor. "Yes, but…" we tell ourselves (and them). "That may be true, but it is *not* the whole picture." This is simply another way of saying *not enough, never enough!*

In theory, we know about basic goodness, or basic intelligence, or common sense, or the grace of God. But to *live* as if these are true of us – well…not so easy.

A MOMENT OF PUSHING THROUGH

Let's recall a time when we *have* demonstrated the opposite of our "not enough." What we are pointing to here is some moment, any moment, when you moved ahead despite your basic mistrust default (some stingy conclusion you held about yourself), even if that mistrust impulse was present and pulsing. For me (Regina), these "push through" moments are regular. As a writer, I admit to generally feeling like a fraud, especially in my younger years (but still). After all, who could dare call herself a writer (or worse, a poet) when confronted with the likes of Joan Didion, or Annie Dillard, or Mary Oliver? Name *your* favorite! But the push-through is that I don't stop writing. In fact, I stretch my comfort zone to dare to coach others in writing. The thoughts of "not good enough" are still there, but I step around them.

For me (Shinay), it's not just a single moment of pushing through. Every day, when I sit in front of my yoga students, a part of me wants to wither and sink into the floor. My Lady Less-Than is ruthless. "Who are you kidding? These people…

they're twice your age! How could you offer anything of substance that they don't already know? Also, your voice is too soft, your words are not…," she taunts. Yet, I am forced to sit still and push through because I know there is another "I" – one who knows a deeper truth. This wiser "I" knows that I have studied, that I have practiced, and that I don't have to pretend to have answers. "Not-knowing" becomes a great strength for me. My fear doesn't go away, I freely admit, but if I can simply expand a bit, I can become empty, transparent, and I'm unable to be hooked by a self-hating "I". In doubting moments I rely on gratitude – recalling how grateful I am for both my mentors and my students and what a privilege it is to offer some small encouragement or guidance to another. I am a student of my students – and grateful for it.

Each of us has a story or stories in which we *have* risked, *have* moved ahead, despite our feared conclusions, our sense of the scarcity of love, our self-doubts and our misgivings. Sharing one or more of these stories with another person can literally warm a room. Try it! Write a letter affirming this truth. By sending a letter to someone else, you can touch a heart. Simply remembering the incident, using it as a point of reference for yourself, is wonderful, too. Such remembrance stirs the heart. Gratitude, like a tiny flame, is kindled. Hearing our friends, our sisters, speak of their push-throughs is a testimony to the power of Woman's love, her persistence, her courage. The more we hear, the more we are touched by the force of gratitude – a "blessing force."

Awakening our gratitude for *what is*, rather than feeding the habit of *what isn't*, is not a simple practice. We are working against centuries of cultural conditioning and a lifetime of reinforcement. It helps so much to have the support of others and the inspiration of their examples. The commitment to re-engage our own courage and strength, to practice saying, "Step over, move on; I bless what is," builds personal power. While *not good enough* doesn't disappear, up-leveling it to the domain of gratitude can become a way of life.

A BLESSING WALK

One afternoon many years ago, during a little retreat that I (Regina) took for a few days before Christmas, I was taking a walk on a dirt road through a pine forest when it started to snow. Fully alone and away from home, and with no one else to talk to for several days, I was so touched ("radically amazed" is a better way to put it) by the beauty of this moment that I ached with it. What to *do* with such amazement? Should I stop and write a poem? Should I call someone on my cell phone and share it? Should I get down on my knees and kiss the earth, or stand up, run around and hug the trees?

In that lucky moment, as mind searched for some way to express these deep feelings, I was hit with...well, an amazing grace. Spontaneously, I found my center of attention within my own eyes, where simply seeing, without commentary, was happening. *Seeing beauty* – witnessing to the wonder of this tiny page of creation that had opened before me – was the only important thing. I wasn't *willing* this to happen, but I was saying Yes to it.

I drank in the beauty through my eyes, and then through my nose, my mouth, my skin. Maybe it was only thirty seconds' worth of drunken gratitude, but I remember it today as clearly as if I were "in" it now. Words too arose spontaneously – words like "thank you, thank you; blessings, blessings; magnificat, magnificat." I didn't plan it.

When mind and memory returned, so did the image of my ninety-year-old mother who had been blind for four years at that point. Next thing I knew, I had concocted a plan to let myself *see* beauty on her behalf. "Hey, Mom, look at this…and this…and that…" In some weird way, unable to explain the technology at play in that moment, I knew she was receiving a blessing through me in all of this. And pretty soon the seeing for her expanded to include lots more folks, like those who were blinded by pain, or rage, or prison confinement, or despair. "Blessing, blessing, blessing," I chanted to myself. Goodness and love, goodness and love, goodness and love to each and all. What a Christmas present!

That's the day I invented the Blessing Walk for myself, and now I pray this way often. Instead of my usual exercise stroll, I can intentionally set out in any direction and "bless" whatever beauty (or pain) I see, on behalf of all. If I pass some other person along the way, I silently bless her or him, too.

The Blessing Walk characterizes a transformed way of life. The usual tendencies of self-absorbed doubt and not enoughness can be "redeemed" as gratitude and blessing become a focus. These amazing graces have literally "saved a wretch like me"!

Gratitude

If we can stop the self-loathing, or even just diminish it by two percent, our friends would benefit. Our families would thank us. Our beloveds would be able to relax and rejoice more in our company. Self-depreciation makes us brittle and tight. To realize Woman we must expand. Just as our cervix must open wide for birth, we must stretch with gratitude in order to live fully and not become hardened by self-hate.

– Shinay

A LITANY OF BLESSING

Confronting self-hatred head on rarely changes anything, as you've probably seen clearly by now. Building a different body, a body of blessings and gratitude, on the other hand, may be an entry into self-appreciation, albeit through a side door. The Blessing Walk is a daring practice in places where lots of other people are around, like in a subway, in an airplane, on a busy city street. It is daring because it invites you to soften toward others, and to stretch the imaginary boundaries of your love and caring. You can take this practice to the grocery store. You can go to a concert or movie and enact a Blessing Walk through the arena or theatre at intermission. Imagine that! Instead of looking at the other concertgoers with a critical eye, you can spread blessing through your eyes, opening your heart to others in their pain…and allowing yourself also to share their joy.

You Never Know

"If you were to tell me one piece of advice for living well, what would it be?" I (Shinay) asked her.

I was speaking to a dear friend of mine – a woman not much older than myself – who has Lupus, has suffered multiple brain hemorrhages, and is currently struggling with extreme health complications.

"I'll give you two bits of hot stuff," Helen said. "First, always be kind to everyone you encounter everywhere, because you never know what someone is going through. I'm always exhausted and in maximum pain even though I don't 'look' sick. So, I instantly assume that someone else could be in the exact same boat as I am. Second, I acknowledge everyone I come across, even if it's with just a smile."

A Blessing Walk is uniquely revelatory in the wilderness where blessings can be made upon trees, rocks, cacti, rabbits or squirrels, even insects. It can be made to air, to water, to fire, to wind. Some of us love to create rituals. Blessing rituals are particularly easy: simply "bless" all the elements of nature wherever you are. How about even blessing weather that is fierce or that causes discomfort? That would be a new experience.

A Blessing Walk can be done without ever leaving your chair or your couch. Haven't contemplative monks and nuns, and great visionaries, done this for ages? You can bless all who visit you, all who call you, and all who text or e-mail you. You can make a list of all the people in your life – family, friends, enemies, coworkers – and take one blessing breath on behalf of each one. (I (Regina) suggested a similar practice to a dear artist friend who is essentially housebound due to illness. As my friend strings the beads she uses in her bead sculptures, she blesses each one as a suffering child somewhere in the world. Others don't ever need to know what you are doing on their behalf. Consider this practice as the offering of a member of a secret blessing-force society. It's just radical enough for some of us!

While it is generally easier to remember to bless when things are beautiful and great, it is even more important to bless illnesses, hurting bodies, dark times, discouraging breakdowns, failures, and the sense of not being good enough – as long-term or as fleeting as these experiences or moods may be. We can bless the people who have annoyed us, threatened us, interrupted us, scared us. In our prayers we can bless our own thoughts – as stupid, distracted, or nonsensical as they may seem. We can definitely bless emotions: good, bad or otherwise. Bless desires, dreams, hopes, fears – your own and those of your closest ones or partner. Bless others not because you are trying to change them. Simply stay with blessing *what is* and see where that takes you.

It is so important to bless the body (your body, too!). A pregnant woman might easily think of blessing her infant in utero but may neglect to bless her own aching back, her swollen feet and toes, her indigestion, her dry lips or rough hands. The parts that are hurting and crying out need our blessing attention more than the parts that are silent. Blessing becomes an alternative to worry (well, at least we try to use it that way). Blessing ourselves and sending loving attention and breath to a part of the body that is alerting us to some need is crucial. Personally, I (Regina) admit the need to bless my liver, stomach, breasts – any areas where I hold fear and darkness. Imagine putting a smile on the flesh of your thighs, on those facial wrinkles, your thinning hair. There is just so much to bless.

I Am Enough

Each morning as I (Shinay) massage my skin with sesame oil, I repeat a mantra, a prayer, to deepen my gratitude for the gift of this body and this life: "I am enough. I have a lot of love in my life. I am beautiful, whole, complete and perfect already. I am enough. I give thanks." I take time to thank my body. I thank the day, the morning light, the heater in my house, the rug beneath my feet and the sesame oil in my hands. There is no special protocol for blessing and gestures of gratitude.

We can also do blessings on each other now and then, gently placing our hands on shoulders, skull, feet, clavicle... praying for one another.

Blessing is synonymous with prayer, and for some of us it can become a form of activism. We can start with ourselves, then extend the blessing to the folks who live next door, to the neighborhood, the town, the city, the country…the whole world. What about blessing our president, too, whether we like her/ him or not? The president needs our blessing, and so do world leaders. Why? Because whether we feel compassionate toward them or not, we know they suffer. Just like we do, and probably more. Who knows, you might even find yourself blessing rebels and revolutionaries − even those who perform atrocities. Your blessing does not approve their evils. Your blessing sends softening to their hearts. Bless the victims of such evils. Bless soldiers and police. Bless anyone you have any prejudice toward.

Here's a unique subject to consider: what about blessing your past life? How about using your breath as the blessing carrier, breathing upon the event of your own birth and upon your mother as she endured the process, along with the doctors or nurses who assisted her? Funny, but we may never before have thought of those people. They may be long departed from this Earth. Since blessing lives in a dimension outside of space and time, who knows what this merits?

Breathe blessings upon your childhood, on both your parents, on siblings, aunts and uncles, and all the people who raised you. You can bless the pets who gave you so much comfort when nobody else did. Bless the schools you attended, your old teachers (Wow, don't you hope they're happy now?), the friends of your early years. We can also bless the dozens of intersections along our path with another, be they lover, friend or mentor.

Perhaps you're getting the feel for this practice. Hopefully, you see how it alters the focus of not enough as it becomes a form of gifting the whole creation.

Writing blessing prayers is a most powerful practice. Keeping a small blessing book in which you record your prayers can be useful, too. One of our friends suggested that we bless our approaching death, as it is never too soon or too late to be preparing. Also, we can bless the death and other transitioning processes of those we love.

Finally, since we all – writers and readers – are involved in this book because we share the issue of self-hatred, how about blessing that tendency? How about blessing self-doubts and comparisons with others, and bad judgments of ourselves? Let's bless our sins, real or imagined.

What do you say?

GRATITUDE / BLESSING / JOY / HAPPINESS

By now you may have heard about the practice of keeping a Gratitude Journal. A lot has been written about it online and in the popular press in recent years. Seems there's actual research that indicates the benefits of keeping a Gratitude Journal – benefits like greater happiness, better relationships, improved health, career boosts, strengthened positive emotions, more life resilience.

Author Elizabeth Gilbert (*Big Magic*, 2015) suggests keeping what she calls a "Happiness Jar." I (Shinay) have started calling mine my "Joy Jar." At the end of each day, I write down one (or more) things that brought me joy in the last twenty-four hours. I invite you to use this same idea for a "Blessing Jar." Simply write the names of people you wish to bless on a small paper or card and put the note in the Blessing Jar. You might also write down little affirmations, prayers, or whatever you're grateful for. Then, at the end of the year, you might take them out, read them, and burn them in a ritual burning.

A Bit of Research

Gratitude, it turns out, makes you happier and healthier. If you invest in a way of seeing the world that is mean and frustrated, you're going to get a world that is . . . well . . . more mean and frustrating. But if you can find any authentic reason to give thanks, anything that is going right with the world or your life, and put your attention there, statistics say you're going to be better off.
– http://www.huffingtonpost.com/ocean-robbins/having-gratitude-_b_1073105.html

Gratitude enhances empathy and reduces aggression. Grateful people are more likely to behave in a pro-social manner, even when others behave less kindly, according to a 2012 study by the University of Kentucky. Study participants who ranked higher on gratitude scales were less likely to retaliate against others, even when given negative feedback. They experienced more sensitivity and empathy toward other people and a decreased desire to seek revenge.
– http://www.forbes.com/sites/amymorin/2014/11/23/7-scientifically-proven-benefits-of-gratitude-that-will-motivate-you-to-give-thanks-year-round/

Grateful people – those who perceive gratitude as a permanent trait rather than a temporary state of mind – have an edge on the not-so-grateful when it comes to health, according to University of California, Davis, psychology professor Robert Emmons' research on gratitude. "Gratitude research is beginning to suggest that feelings of thankfulness have tremendous positive value

in helping people cope with daily problems, especially stress," Emmons told WebMD. In the same article, Elizabeth Heubeck wrote, "It's no secret that stress can make us sick, particularly when we can't cope with it. It's linked to several leading causes of death, including heart disease and cancer, and claims responsibility for up to 90% of all doctor visits. Gratitude, it turns out, can help us better manage stress."
– http://www.webmd.com/women/features/gratitute-health-boost

"Not Enough" for the World

We see the world's tragedies and the vast expanse of human suffering everywhere, and immediately. With so much media input of this type, we can easily feel overwhelmed, filled with a sense of helplessness and hopelessness. We *get* that the planet is in trouble, we *see* the fate of dispossessed people everywhere. We ache with the sense that we (personally and collectively) are *not doing enough* to end poverty, global warming, child abuse, religious violence. "All life is suffering" is the first noble truth of the Buddha. We attempt to deal with that truth as best we can.

Still, goodness and beauty and a stand for happiness and the well-being of others is everywhere around us. And we do tend to miss *what is* – the good, beautiful, happy – focused as we are on what isn't. Which is exactly what we do within our own minds in our judgments of others, and of ourselves, in believing the lie of never enough.

Let's face it, we are a "fix it" people! We declare war on cancer, war on drugs, an end to hunger…Fix, fix, fix – there is no end to it. Look at your daily life and see if you too are not infected with the great "fixer" disease. Fixing education for young children? Fixing homelessness? Fixing your daughter's marriage? Fixing your husband's wardrobe? We want to make the world right; we want an end to pain. We want safety, predictability, and closure. We want complete and unblemished "good enough" in all circumstances, and for everyone.

Well, guess what. It isn't going to happen. Wake up. The attempt to fix something and the anxiety of not being able to fix everything is what we've been dealing with for countless years. "If only I had more/ better/ different...," "If only I could...," "If only it wasn't..."

Dedication to practicing Radical Move 7 requires a deep dive into the cold waters of unfixable life – your own and that around you. *Please* don't read this as a call to passivity or inaction. Rather, see it as a way to move forward by plunging underneath; see it as a call to practical work on yourself that leads to genuine compassion for the brokenness of all the world's stuff (including your own). Suffering was, is, and ever will be. *And*, genuine compassion still moves us to serve and love, and to forgive, and to build and create and celebrate, even if the world never gets better. Because love can't help it.

This call to gratitude for *what is* instead of obsession with and fear of *what isn't* frees us up (at least a bit) from the illusion that a whole lot is going to change, and immediately. Hear this plea as a clarion call to come home to your own basic goodness. "Good enough" begins at home, and from there radiates in all directions. You become an effective activist rather than a mere fixer when your service flows from the mood of "witness and bless," rather than from "change or die!"

> *Ours is not the task of fixing the entire world all*
> *at once, but of stretching out to mend the part of*
> *the world that is within our reach. Any small,*

> calm thing that one soul can do to help another
> soul, to assist some portion of the poor suffering
> world, will help immensely.
>
> — Clarissa Pinkola Estes

EXERCISE – *Questions to Consider, Talk About, Write About*

1. Would it make any difference if someone said to you, "I thank you"; "I remember you"; "I see who you are"; "I'm so grateful that you are in my life"?

2. How does blessing show up in your life right now?

3. What do you want to bless? And how do you want to do it?

4. What's your **Moment of Pushing Through?** Describe it.

5. List the illnesses, physical hurts, dark times, discouraging breakdowns, failures, self-doubts, comparisons with others, bad judgments of yourself, "sins" (real or imagined), ways in which you are "not good enough." Grieve for them, feel what they still evoke for you, breathe with them, and bless them. The process of grieving requires blessing as a way to transition. Are you ready? Write them down.

6. How might you bless your body?

7. How might you bless your childhood, your parents, siblings, aunts and uncles, and all the people who raised you?

Learn to Fly

Regina: As a child, I frequently touched upon something magical, something I couldn't describe, something that felt like *forever and ever*. Ecstasy with the first snowfall. A spontaneous arising of joy as I danced through the house. Something like that. A brief glimpse, perhaps, that everything around me *was* magical. Somehow I knew there *was* wonder; there were stories of things or people changing into something remarkable and happy. I sensed the truth of this in my childlike way.

Shinay: I grew up knowing that fairies were real. Even though I never caught sight of any, I would build gardens and playgrounds for them in my mother's flowerbeds using leaves, rocks, and twigs. I also grew up hearing *leelas*, the Sanskrit word for stories of "Divine play." A *leela* is another way to describe creative play brought about through Grace – unexpected, wondrous, out of time. These *leelas* were not made up. They were true stories (my favorite kind) about people who had traveled to foreign countries and met someone by chance who then directed them to meet another person, and so on, ultimately unfolding a tangible magic for the traveler.

I used to have reoccurring nightmares of volcanoes. The last time I had this dream, the nightmare turned into a magnificent scene where I could fly, saving my family and friends by lifting them up and moving with them out of harm's way. I still remember and connect with the power I knew in this dream.

Kids are organically innocent. It's no wonder their dreams of transformation are so compelling. For them, anything is possible. Caterpillars into butterflies? Certainly! Cinderella into the perfect princess? Right on! Wendy thinking happy thoughts and flying off to Never Never Land? Sure!

The Radical Move that we invite you into here is a reconnection with a deep longing that lies within the human heart. Let's call it the urge to fly. Or let's call it a dream of transformation. Or simply a longing for truth, or God, or your deepest heart's desire, or love, or making a difference. Call it an intuitive knowing of Buddha nature, or the Christ consciousness, or identify it simply as the pull to soar that overtakes some of us when we watch a raven or a hawk playing on the wind currents. Whatever description you might use for your pull, your longing, or whatever you want to *make up* now, even if the words don't exactly fit – such dreams and longings are important. They work us. Quietly, in the dark, often in silence. Remembered, they connect us with the mystery – *the* Mystery – that surrounds us. Start a conversation about *this* with your friends.

This connection to mystery and magic moves us into another domain, outside the tight box of *never good enough*. In the realm of the spirit in flight, or the magical world of transformational miracles, *never good enough* doesn't have legs. In touch with such magic, timelessness, and spaciousness, radiant possibility abides. Limiting beliefs about self are simply too dense and heavy to get off the ground here.

FLYING IS REAL

The shamanic truth that underlies the Peter Pan story is deeply significant. People *can* fly! They *have* flown, by the power of directed attention and in states of radical dreaming. They fly because they are not merely bags of bones shuffling around on an inert grassland. They fly because they are spirits/souls having a human experience, and they have a big mission to do here.

Along the way, however, many of them, and us, have been misled in our desire to "fly." Said another way, we have allowed ourselves to be waylaid from our heart's deepest desire. We may have tried skydiving or taken up some other extreme sport in our attempt to alter our consciousness and move us out of the mundane for a while. We may have tried to fly by smoking a lot of dope, drinking a lot of beer, having a lot of sex, or by fasting, detoxing, or exercising endlessly. Sometimes these behaviors have worked to briefly satisfy the urge toward transcendence; sometimes they have only increased the desire for more of the same addictive substance or activity.

We all must explore – and tell the truth about – such thwarted attempts at flying for ourselves. And we will! Why? Because without verifying the truth through our own experience, we will never really learn. We will only hear the exhortations of others about what works for them, or what "should" work for everybody, as criticism or preaching. We may then turn off help, and hope, putting our dreams and longings aside. Left too long on the shelf, our dreams will start to fade.

The "flying" that Radical Move 8 relates to is the "flight home," back to the pure and innocent heart, the deepest longing, the *Know Thyself* of all the ages and sages, and the truth of Woman. The wilder the world becomes "out there," the more vital it is to learn how to fly home; the more essential it is to find out who we are, and what we *really* want, in all the chaos and clamor. The louder become the voices of *never enough, never good enough* – and make no mistake about it, they are everywhere, under deceptively soothing pretexts – the more critical it is that we land (if only for a few moments each day) in a place in which Basic Goodness, Intrinsic Dignity, and Love and Deep Longing as the Ground of Being are the road markers.

How are these words we just used striking you as you read them? Do they draw forth some tears, some sadness, some hopefulness? Do they cause any physical sensation in the body? At the heart? In the gut? Even if you can't "believe" them with your rational thought, are they moving you in some way? Can you intuit something about their reality? If so, you are being touched by *dharma* – the teachings of truth. If not, try to forestall drawing conclusions about this, accept yourself, and simply read on.

Most of us live in locations that are so full of electromagnetic interference patterns that it is difficult for the body to ever fully relax. We use technological gadgets (some have called them electronic hand-held vampires) to search for answers to everything, or connections to everyone. But no amount of surfing the Net will bring the body into genuine alignment with itself. No Google search will ever satisfactorily answer the questions: Who am I? What is Woman? How can I live out my destiny? For this you need time, space, slowing down, silence and attention.

A genuine conversation in which possibilities for flying are put forth with a trusted other is one way to get to the runway. We've suggested this approach in several places throughout the book. Beyond the *blah blah blah*, we've invited you to articulate with a friend or write about your deepest heart's desire.

MEDITATION / CONTEMPLATION PRACTICE

In this Radical Move we propose another way to learn to fly: through meditation or contemplation (in any of a wide variety of forms). Meditation as we will speak of it is a chance to stop long enough for destiny to find us; for Woman to reveal herself to us; and for *Who am I?* to be converted to *Who I am!* With this Radical Move we recommend a flight into solitude (if only for a day or two) as a way to really rest, get your bearings on the inner compass, and listen for the next step (the next Radical Move) your heart is directing you to.

These methods of flight preparation (meditation and retreating to solitude) are among the best-kept secrets on the planet today. While from every direction you are being seduced into believing that "more is better" in your quest for happiness, we're here to testify that actually "less is more." Becoming lighter is the easiest way to achieve takeoff. And *less* (in the sense of focus on what is essential) is the remedy for never enough. *Less* is the antidote for the poison in the lie of *never good enough.*

Meditation as we present it here is not something religious per se, even though for some of us it quickly evolves into a type of prayer. It is much more about taking the flight that brings you home – to the naked now of your own body, to your breath; to the immediacy of the moment and the day ahead; to your deepest wish, your aim, your dedication, your dream…and also to your fears. (You didn't think we would venture forth into some new atmosphere without them, too, did you?)

Meditation/contemplation for us is about a radical, albeit gentle, confrontation with the illusions that fill the mind, distracting us from the possibilities of fulfilling higher purpose – that truest dream we talked about in previous chapters. Meditation is a primary and dynamic means of challenging the lie of *never good enough.*

Our minds…sigh. It sure is noisy some days. My mind and intellect have been such gifts in my *life*

and on this journey. And, there are times when
my focus of leading from the mind has constricted
and masculinized me. When I was in graduate
school I was rigid, and thought I could think my
way through all of life; I thought I could control
it all to avoid my own suffering. My mind and the
confusion of my thoughts was just so loud: the
thoughts, the judgments, the self-critique, the self-
loathing. So little of it was relevant or true. Maybe
none of it was. Yet my mind was so ridiculously
noisy, taking in so much information that I was
allowing to take me in quite the wrong direction.
Meditation and sadhana were a joy to me because
they helped to quiet my mind and helped to loosen
the hold of the negative thought patterns. What
a gift this has been to quiet the doubts and self-
loathing through the recitation of her mantras and
her names.

    – Aditi Devi, *In Praise of Adya Kali*

Books that teach meditation practice (for beginners or in
depth) are available from many sources, and we will list a few
you might enjoy at the end of the book. Teachers of meditation
are also available, either in person or through online courses.
Groups that meditate together are springing up in cities and
towns everywhere. Most yoga classes will include an introduction
to some type of meditation practice, using breath awareness or
focused attention. The possibilities today are numerous. If you
need help in this regard, hold the highest intention for what
you want, and then ask around. For those of you who have little
or no experience in the practice, and even those who do, a few
basic points and a few basic types of meditation practice, held

within our context of confronting the lie of *never good enough*, are worth considering.

Breath/Thought Awareness Practice

First: *Maintain a posture that connects heaven and earth, in and through you.* Your true nature demands it. Begin by sitting like the queen or grand lady that you are. In the Buddhist tradition it is said that when you sit in meditation you *are* the Buddha. From the Christian tradition it is believed that any attempt at contemplation or prayer is actually God Itself inspiring and generating that prayer in and through you. Regardless of what goes through your mind, regardless of the agitation of feelings in your gut, you can enact the Goddess Alive by simply sitting still with dignity. And don't miss this suggestion for stillness, please. Even if you can remain "still" only for five to ten minutes, it is a worthy pursuit. While walking meditation is awesome, too, and running with your dog may be a chance to celebrate life, there is a unique nectar generated in the still body that will only be tasted by those who try it. *Be still and know that I Am God* (Psalm 46, verse 10) is no joke.

Second: *Breath is the objective (i.e., without judgment) action of life maintenance, connecting you with all living creatures.* Use the breath as a focusing device. Here, now, alive. As you breathe, with even minimal attention to your breath, you are allowing sacred Life Force (call it Holy Spirit, Goddess, Nonjudgmental Love) to fill your body, to enrich and empower you. You *have* thoughts, but you *are not* your thoughts or feelings of *never good enough*. Become the breathing. Use the breath to rest in and simply remember who you really are, not separate from that sacred source, that Life Force.

Third: *"Take a friendly attitude toward your thoughts"* as *they come and go.* This advice comes from Tibetan meditation master Chögyam Trungpa Rinpoche. The point is that each and every thought is just a blip on the screen, with no reality in the moment except as a phenomenon, based in a memory. It is an invitation to *lightly* observe how your mind works, and *lightly* return to what is really present here and now – that is, to your posture and your breath.

When we say that meditation practice challenges the lie of *never good enough*, we are hitting closer to the nerve of truth than in all our previous Radical Moves. Meditation practice reveals skewed thinking patterns, the endless internal tape loops and tired old songs of defense against love that have been circulating in our heads *ad infinitum*. Just begin.

Fourth: *Continue returning to the breath, to the center, again and again.*

Meditation of the Heart Practice

This approach to meditation uses a very simple visualization to generate a sense of love within. This one was given to homeless women in several homeless shelters in California by my (Regina's) friend, author and therapist Anne Scott. It is found in her new book called *Finding Home*. As short as it is, it has the power to open the heart and touch us profoundly. We are happy to share it with you here.

> Become aware of your breath, in and out, like gentle waves at the ocean.
>
> Now, think of someone you love. Or a time you felt moved by nature, like watching a sunset or standing at the ocean.
>
> However you feel this love, which is unique for each of us, place this feeling in your heart.

> As thoughts arise in the mind, just drop them into the heart, one by one, like dropping pebbles into a pond.

Sit in silence with this experience for ten minutes or so. Take a moment to write or share what has occurred for you.

Metta Practice

In the book *Radiant Mind* (articles compiled by Jean Smith), meditation teacher and author Sharon Salzberg instructs:

> In metta practice, we direct lovingkindness toward ourselves and then, in a sequence of expansion, towards somebody we love already, somebody we are neutral towards, somebody we have difficulty with, and ultimately toward all beings everywhere without distinction. . .
>
> In metta practice people are amazed to find out that they have a capacity for lovingkindness, both for themselves and for others. Due to our past conditioning, many of us do not trust our capacity to love...We discover that we can indeed love and that everything comes back to love.

Starting My Day

I (Shinay) like to get up early in the quiet dawn to start my day before the day starts without me.

Most days I try to wake up naturally because the sound of an alarm makes me forget my dreams. I like remembering my dreams and I don't like the feeling of being jolted awake. I say a prayer so that the first words out of my mouth are gratitude

– this sets the pace/tone for the rest of my day (or at least that's the idea). I cuddle up next to my husband and kiss his eyes, forehead, and shoulders, whispering, "I love you." Occasionally he's up before me.

After I eliminate my bowels, I'm ready to sit in silence (aka meditation). If silent sitting doesn't happen right away and I start checking my phone and e-mails and planning for the day, it's hard to gather the energy back and sit down, quietly, without fidgeting. It's hard to stop that momentum of the day.

Right food, exercise, and meditation are essential for my ideal day. Meditation clears space. As my Sanskrit teacher said, "Meditation is like taking yourself on a first date." I firmly believe this. Every time I sit in meditation, I practice dating myself. "Something" usually "happens" after the thirty-minute mark, much like on a first date: there's either a connection, or you know right away that you never want to see the person again. Sometimes my back and legs start to ache. Sometimes my nose will start to drip…but I'll make myself "stay at the table"; after all, I'm on a date!

The key *for me* is to not give in to every itch or uncomfortable sensation. When I relax just enough to keep an upright posture and let the rest of my body release tension, I'm able to simply BE, and I can tune into the constant, irritating (often debilitating and deceitful) mind-chatter or "mind-olog," as I like to call it.

I've noticed that, over the years, sitting in silence *consistently* gives me a literal pause in my day to focus on just breathing. In doing this, I notice that I'm much more able to become aware of my breath *throughout* my day and, as a result, I'm more able to be responsible rather than reactive in any given situation. (Understand the difference?)

My body knows the benefit of meditation practice; my mind too recognizes the benefit. My partner likes it when I'm less reactive. My friends notice that I'm more grounded. In twenty years I hope to still be practicing meditation and finding new levels of intimacy with myself.

In general, I don't make a big deal about sitting down to meditate. Sure, I might light a candle or burn some incense, but often I just sit in the same spot (this is important because it gives the brain a trigger to "sit here, now"), wrap up in a blanket or shawl, tuck my legs underneath me, and stick a cushion under my bum. I feel most comfortable sitting on the floor, but a chair works just fine, in my opinion, as long as the spine is straight and the rest of the body can relax. I set an alarm clock so I'm not constantly checking the time, and then close my eyes.

The discipline of sitting in silence every day seems to be developing kindness in me (kindness is the new sexy!) because I can make better distinctions between intelligent body-mind action and egoic body-mind action. The practice of sitting in silence is luxurious, really. I've even started to train myself to arrive ten minutes early for appointments just so I can sit in silence before the other person arrives. (Previously, and you can ask my husband, I had a tendency to rush places and arrive just in the nick of time, not allowing myself any "breathing room.") This new habit of arriving early helps me to actually create a more intentional, energy-filled, sacred, present space for myself and the other person or people I'm going to meet. "Waiting" is a great opportunity to meditate.

RETREAT TO SILENCE, SOLITUDE AND SANCTUARY

When we talk about retreat, we are talking about real solitude, not just the fact that you might live alone in a studio apartment in the midst of a city. We're talking about a temporary respite from phones, iPads, computers, shopping, the corner deli, a pile of books you've always wanted to read, a book (or letters) you need to write, visits from friends, kids, jobs that *must* be done. We are talking about radical unplugging.

For us, this venture in unplugging is exciting to imagine, and we know that for some of you it is about as attractive as a dental implant. That's probably because you still believe your mind regarding what's supposed to make you happy, and not remembering how much you want to genuinely fly. That's probably because you're more comfortable with logical excuses than illogical freedom. And, it may simply be that you are not supported or guided/coached in how to make or use retreat as that first or further step off the edge. We get it. We've been there, too.

You *can* make horizontal improvements in overcoming self-hatred without meditation practice or retreat. You *can* get your unmanageable self-loathing messages under control through affirmations and certain kinds of behavioral therapy. You *can* team up with friends who will sit in a circle with you and remind you to "Cut it out!" Yes, yes, yes. All of this is what we have been encouraging for you.

Flying is about something else.

"Flying," as we are presenting it here, is more about jumping off the cliff, facing sure death and then suddenly experiencing yourself as unlimited – by gravity, by the mind, or by the cultural programs that have kept you heavy and safe. It's about knowing yourself as "bigger" or "lighter" or "deeper" than you've previously allowed. Flying happens when we are willing to expose ourselves to the elements (metaphor here!) with little support except our own buoyancy; we then let go and allow ourselves to be carried on the wind!

Truth is, the fear of death, and fear in general, is what keeps us weighted down. The chance of experiencing flying... freedom – the radical truth of who we are – is greatly enhanced when we allow death to be a friend and a mentor. When we take the radical step off the cliff. When we give ourselves the opportunity to "die before you die," as many religious traditions have encouraged us.

We will each die alone. A-L-O-N-E. Retreat practice is a way to practice dying. Retreat practice is a way to "die" before you actually die, and thus to learn that you are eternal...or at least in possession of an eternal "something." Retreat practice is a way to fly vertically, regardless of self-loathing, and even because of it. Self-loathing and self-doubt are perhaps components of the fuel that will propel you. Retreat is potentially a way to experiment with how to digest and use the energy of self-hatred for your transformational purposes.

How? We assert that if you've made it this far in the book you *do* know (or at least intuit) how to explore this inner transformation. You may not be giving yourself the time or space to do this. At the very least, retreat will be a time to develop real questions about how to deal with these issues. Remember, you can only recognize and know the *never good enough* because you already have a sense of what life could be like when *good enough* was fully running the show. It is inner clarity that recognizes when we are in confusion. It is inner goodness that recognizes when we are falling for *the lie of never enough*. Contemplate this seriously.

Don't rush ahead into this retreat step. Consider it for as long as you need to. Talk about it. Express your fears. I (Regina) work part-time at a small retreat center in northern Arizona, and I speak with friends from all over who tell me they couldn't make a formal retreat because they're afraid of boredom, afraid of mountain lions and rattlesnakes, afraid of their own minds, afraid of missing their kids, afraid that their husbands will die of malnutrition while they are away. The list goes on and on.

I tell them, "Great! That's normal," and add that what *will* happen on retreat is more likely *not* what they set up as their fear obstacle. More often, what will arise on retreat will be a surprise. "It will often blindside us," I say. In fact, it is for this reason that I choose to make a retreat year after year, and sometimes a few times in one year. I want to know *Who am I?* as a bodily reality, not some mental notion that will fill in a blank on a questionnaire. I'm willing to risk the boredom and the missing of loved ones.

Courage, dear sisters. Retreat does offer you challenges and struggles. After all, as Buckaroo Banzai says, "No matter where you go, there you are." You are free to go to Hawaii instead. We guarantee that you won't uncover there what you will uncover in a few weeks (or even a few days) of silence, solitude, and sanctuary.

Part of the difficulty with overcoming self-hatred is that we rarely have uninterrupted time to actually listen to the chattering voices and the lies they keep chanting. When there is no one around except you, you get to find out that these lies are disembodied, coming from some old, dusty, scratchy phonograph record in your own head, not from the environment. You get to find out that all your fears are located between your ears. That's something so valuable as to be priceless. We mean it. Don't underestimate this fact.

Will you join the club of the intrepid? Weak in the knees or not.

BABY STEPS

We recommend that you "start small" if you're really freaked out by this idea of a radical retreat. Recently, I (Regina) worked until noon and then drove to a favorite spot in the nearby hills, yoga mat under my arm, water bottle in hand, old rag rug to

A Short Retreat

One Saturday I (Shinay) left my house early. I packed water, food, and a notebook. I left my cell phone at home and hiked to the top of Granite Mountain, one of the major land features in Prescott, Arizona, where I live. It's where the peregrine falcons nest each year and a much sought after rock-climbing destination. It usually takes four hours to hike round trip – top to bottom. I spent eight on that great slab of granite.

It was a mini-retreat, a day on the mountain alone in silence. When I passed other people on the trail I simply smiled and nodded, no need to say anything out loud. It was a time to think, to let my thoughts run wild while my feet and legs and arms kept a steady pace moving me to the top.

The rampage of mental chatter was enough to keep me company. As the trail became steeper and I sucked in breath through my mouth, I settled into a rhythm of placing one foot in front of the other, chock-chock-crunch. I slowly relaxed and became more sensitive to the natural elements. I allowed myself to be bathed by Her.

When I finally reached the top I lingered for hours. I wrote in my notebook and stared off at the horizon. I sat in the shade of an old alligator juniper and allowed myself the time and space to just *be* – without an agenda or plan, or any expectation that something would happen up there on the mountain.

Honestly, looking back, my experience wasn't one of serene peace, bliss and total satisfaction. I was uncomfortable. Hot. Winded. I was lonely. I daydreamed and my mind told horror stories about me. I filled one page in my notebook with mostly bullshit. I didn't have any profound realizations. AND it was worth it. Days like that are important to me because, just like meditation, they are a way to get to know myself a little better.

sit on. I spent three hours with no agenda except to sit and wait. With great pleasure I can report to you that…nothing happened! Nonetheless, flying took place in the emptiness.

Sometimes these retreats are frustrating, sometimes they are ecstatic. But the gift to yourself is that you are building a body of courage, a body of wisdom, a body of self-appreciation by abandoning yourself to timelessness and emptiness. Out of these ground-level conditions, compassion grows. Shinay and I can attest that we almost always come back from retreat with softness and forgiveness for ourselves, and love for others. Forgiveness will ever soften the sharp edges of self-hatred.

Be creative in finding a time, a place, and a method for your own retreat. Look back at Move 4, where we make *A Radical Suggestion* for a short retreat in your own home. Follow this guideline if that's all you are ready for now. Find a friend who has some experience in this domain and get the help and encouragement you need.

A good book to use as a guide during any solitary retreat is one that will consistently bring you back to the recognition of basic goodness, the antidote to *never good enough*. In this next section, we share a taste of this work with you. Use the following quotes to spark further discussions with your sisters and friends. Use them for meditation, or to inspire reflection and writing.

Blessings on your way.

Basic Goodness as a Way of Life

The excerpts that follow are taken from one of our favorite books, *Shambhala: Sacred Path of the Warrior,* by the Tibetan Buddhist master Chögyam Trungpa Rinpoche.

> If we are willing to take an unbiased look, we will find that, in spite of all our problems and confusion,

all our emotional and psychological ups and downs, there is something basically good about our existence as human beings. We have moments of basic non-aggression and freshness...it is worthwhile to take advantage of these moments...we have an actual connection to reality that can wake us up and make us feel basically, fundamentally good. (29-33)

...when you relax more and appreciate your body and mind, you begin to contact the fundamental notion of basic goodness in yourself. So it is extremely important to be willing to open yourself to yourself. Developing tenderness towards yourself allows you to see both your problems and your potential accurately. You don't feel that you have to ignore your problems or exaggerate your potential. That kind of gentleness towards yourself and appreciation of yourself is very necessary. It provides the ground for helping yourself and others. (35-36)

The way to begin is with ourselves. From being open and honest with ourselves, we can also learn to be open with others. So we can work with the rest of the world, on the basis of the goodness we discover in ourselves. Therefore, meditation practice is regarded as a good and in fact excellent way to overcome warfare in the world: our own warfare as well as greater warfare. (41)

9
A RADICAL MOVE BEYOND

Feed the Longing

Okay, so maybe we misled you, a little bit. Haven't you recognized already that there must be many more than Eight Moves available in this challenge? Since you've stayed the course, however, we're going to assume that you find this process useful, so we dare to offer one more essential Move here, just for you. You'll discover a bunch of auxiliary just-for-fun moves in the Appendix.

> *I must listen to the voices of dissent within myself, because a "no" or a "not enough" could just be the beginning of my conversation, not the end. Realizing that I have been lying to myself is the start of something new. The hankering after fullness, for "enoughness," is, at core, none other than my longing for something ultimate – whether I call it the Great Love or Divinity/ Goddess/Oneness. This "longing" should never be quieted or filled. This is part of the ultimate paradox; it's part of what makes the Universe unfold endlessly – light/dark; up/down; yes/no – on and on.*
>
> *– Shinay*

By now you've noted our stand, again and again: that the obsession with *never good enough* is obsession with a lie. Here, as we conclude, we'd like to make a small but vital distinction in this whole challenge. We recognize, as Shinay has articulated so clearly above, that there is another type of obsession, which frankly needs a better name. The great spiritual traditions have assigned a name to it: *longing*. Their truest wisdom-seekers assert that longing is a good thing, an urgency within the human heart to realize the truth of life, or love, or reality. Said another way, it is that urgency that keeps us hungry for "ever more," but not "more" in the sense of a quantity of assurance, or possession of something. Rather, a "more" in the dimension of Being, not the dimension of having.

The great poet Kabir asserts that it is the *longing* that does all the work of revealing truth. The more intense the longing, the greater the possibility of revelation. "Look at me and you will see a slave of that intensity," Kabir says.

If we are to trust this thread of the wisdom traditions, then the longing is a necessity, and will hopefully never end. We will never "have" enough "good" because we already *are* it, and our longing is not for quantity but for realization of our already present condition.

The longing for *ever the good* is a longing for Truth. And this truest longing endures unless we deliberately decide to switch on our life's Cruise Control or the Numb-Out Program. In which case, we can coast or be dragged to the graveyard. On the other hand, genuine longing (longing for the good) will forever get stronger if we have the highest intention to use our precious life to its maximum potential.

Stop here! Another distinction is in order. We're not talking about maximum potential as in a live-life-to-the-hilt mentality that requires climbing mountains, traveling to far corners of the Earth, tasting every rare wine in France, burning the candle at both ends in everything, or playing tennis well into our nineties. None of these activities is unworthy, and if they give delight you should go after them. Still, they may all be accomplished and yet leave us full of self-hatred and plagued by that sense of needing more. This "more" is not the longing we are aiming at.

The deep longing of the highest human potential has to do with a hunger for the truth, and an opening to love, again and again. It may involve starting from zero, as a beginner, each day, and rededicating ourselves to the endless adventure all throughout the day; that adventure being the exploration into our Truest Nature.

> *There was never any more inception than there is now,*
> *Nor any more youth or age than there is now.*
> *And will never be any more perfection than there is now,*
> *Nor any more heaven or hell than there is now.*
> *Urge and urge and urge,*
> *Always the procreant urge of the world.*
> — Walt Whitman

We encourage you to journey more deeply into your own deepest longing. Write about it. Talk about it, beyond the *blah blah blah*. We encourage you to explore the distinction between "wanting" or "having" and "longing" and to discuss your thoughts and feelings about this distinction with those you love and trust. We encourage you to write, refining your truest heart's desire, over and over, day in and day out. We encourage you to clarify your intention. We encourage you to start from nothing, from not-knowing, from *beginning again* in mind and heart. We encourage you to never stop, and to approach all of this gently.

EXERCISE – *Last Questions for Human Beings*

Please consider seriously the questions that follow, which we don't ask flippantly. Work with them, let them gnaw at you. Don't give up on them with some superficial (cheap!) closure.

Give yourself all the time you need to work on these questions. We're not kidding. These questions can actually transform your life. Take them to heart. Be diligent. When you get stuck, start looking around and listening for guides, teachers, friends who can assist you.

Have fun.

THE QUESTIONS

When you say, "I hate myself" or "I doubt myself" or "I am not enough," *exactly* who or what are you referring to by "I" and by "hate"? by "my" and "self"? by "doubt," "am," and "not enough"?

Unravel the tangle you've made of the words you are using to express the self-hatred you say you have. Define your terms. Better yet, *feel into* your terms. Write about these. Discuss them.

Good luck.

CLOSING PRAYER

Here's a prayer that we both honor. Please use it if it appeals to you. What it means is that you are essentially whole and perfect, just as you are; that you have never been separate from Perfection, from Love, and that any apparent diminishment is illusory. Perfection and Love abide eternally in its fullness. All is one, all is peace.

We all love you.

ॐ

Om Puurnnam-Adah Puurnnam-Idam,
Puurnnaat-Purnnam-Udacyate [uuh da shee-at-ay]
Puurnnashya, Puurnnam-Aadaaya,
Puurnnam-Eva-Avashissyate

Om, Shaantih Shaantih Shaantih

Translation

Om, *That* is Perfect, *This* also is Perfect,
From the Perfect springs the Perfect,
Taking the Perfect from the Perfect,
Only the Perfect Remains.

Om, Peace, Peace, Peace.

More Radical Moves

Here are some adjunct Radical Moves that you might make, alone or with your group of friends. Any of them might evolve into something much larger or deeper than you initially suspect. The important thing is to relax and have fun in the process!

You might also consider these as additions to your Delight List – ways to play and get back into the art of your heart.

- Write your own book about challenging self-hatred and how you've addressed it; post your book online.
- Spend a day in a shopping mall and don't buy anything. Watch other women and watch your own thoughts. Keep a small notebook in which to record your reflections.
- Get a group of women-friends together and play nonstop dance music in a safe and private place. Dance to the point of exhaustion. (Keep the music going for three hours, even if you can't stay in motion the whole time.) Gather together and ask each other the question *What is Woman?* when the time is up.
- Take a hike, a camp-out, a cruise, a rafting trip with one or more women-friends in which the purpose of the trip is to challenge self-hatred. Meet whenever you wish and share what you're learning.
- Start wearing a WASH button (make your own) and engage in generative conversation with everyone who asks you about it. (*See* Radical Move 2)

- Declare an "International No Self-Hatred Day," applying this intention in your body, mind, and emotions; and declare your home to be a "Hatred-Free Space" for the day. Invite a friend to dinner and tell her what you've done and how it worked out.

- Begin a prayer vigil (lasting for nine days) on behalf of suffering women in another part of the world, and pray for them as if your prayers were really making a positive difference in their lives. Find images of these women in magazines or on the Net, and place them in a sacred shrine in your house, or wherever you will see them. Record your own reflections before and after this nine-day period relevant to the self-hatred arising in your own life.

- Sit with a group of young children who are playing and look for early signs of self-doubt and self-hatred, if any.

- Talk to mothers/other mothers about the Never-Perfect-Mom syndrome that so many have been infected with. Explore the high price that is being paid for carrying this disease.

- Find an older woman and interview her about how self-hatred has or has not infected her life.

- Change your physical perspective dramatically by climbing a mountain, a tree, or a tower. Get up high enough to shift your point of view. Look out over the world from this vantage point. Reflect on what is happening below you: life, death, sex, making food, eating food, togetherness, loneliness, people laughing, crying, breaking up, getting together, loving passionately. Take it all in. Allow time for silence, for being with these creatures below you; and let prayer arise if it does.

- Unplug. Leave technology off, and at home if you are out and about, for an afternoon, a day, a week. Experience life without a buffer. Sit at a cafe and read. Walk down the sidewalk and greet those you pass. Attend to the sensations of existence. Slow down. Write about what happens.

- Make a pilgrimage, even if only to a special rock in your back yard or a blooming tree in your neighborhood – or go so far as to a holy land in another country. It doesn't matter where you go just as long as you travel with the intent to *receive*. This is the way of a pilgrim. You are not to take, not to intrude. Instead, you are to listen, get humble, make an offering.

- Teach or give a talk about something you're good at. Dig deep, past the surface of your fear and self-doubt to a place where you know truth rests. From that place, begin to speak.

- Make food and invite your family, friends, neighbors. There is nothing more rewarding than to feed others. Make food as an offering of a piece of your heart, a piece of your being. There is potentially great joy in creating and then inviting others into your world. Create and then step aside, open the door, and let others feast.

- Fail at something, especially something big! If you aren't *yet*, you probably aren't taking any risks. We your sisters and mothers and friends and children need you to quit the club of perfection and join the ranks of real Woman. We have a job to do here, in risking and failing and moving forward with dignity and sharpened intention. The entire world, of loved ones and children, needs this from us.

Radical Reading List

Block, Peter. *The Answer to How Is Yes*. San Francisco: Barrett-Koehler, Inc., 2003.

Brown, Brené. *The Gifts of Imperfection: Let Go of Who You Think You're Supposed to Be and Embrace Who You Are*. Canter City, Minnesota: Hazelden, 2010.

Chögyam, Ngakpa. *Journey into Vastness: A Handbook of Tibetan Meditation Techniques*. Billings, Great Britain: Element Books Limited, 1988.

Devi, Aditi. *In praise of Adya Kali: Approaching the Primordial Dark Goddess Through the Song of Her Hundred Names*. Chino Valley, Ariz.: Hohm Press, 2014.

Gilbert, Elizabeth. *Big Magic: Creative Living beyond Fear*. New York: Riverhead Books, 2015.

Maki, Bhavani Sylvia. *The Yogi's Roadmap: The Patanjali Yoga Sutra as a Journey to Self Realization*. Hanalei, Hawaii: Viveka Press, 2013.

Mountain Dreamer, Oriah. *The Invitation*. New York: HarperCollins Publishers, 1995.

Red Hawk. *Self Observation: The Awakening of Consciousness (An Owner's Manual)*. Prescott, Ariz.: Hohm Press, 2009.

Red Hawk. *Self Remembering: The Path to Non-judgmental Love (An Owner's Manual)*. Chino Valley, Ariz.: Hohm Press, 2015.

Ryan, Regina Sara. *Woman Awake*. Prescott, Ariz.: Hohm Press, 1998.

Ryan, Regina Sara. *Igniting the Inner Life*. Prescott, Ariz: Hohm Press, 2009.

Salzberg, Sharon. *Lovingkindness: The Revolutionary Art of Happiness.* Boston: Shambhala, 2002.

Scott, Anne. *Finding Home: Restoring the Sacred to Life - Stories of Women in Homelessness and Transition.* Nicasio, Calif.: Nicasio Press, 2016.

Scott, Anne. *Women, Wisdom & Dreams: The Light of the Feminine Soul.* Nicasio, Calif.: Nicasio Press, 2008.

Sell, Christina. *My Body Is a Temple: Yoga as a Path to Wholeness.* Prescott, Ariz.: Hohm Press, 2011.

Strayed, Cheryl. *Wild.* New York: Alfred A. Knopf, a division of Random House, Inc., 2012.

Thomas, Lalitha. *Waking to Ordinary Life.* Prescott, Ariz.: Hohm Press, 2011.

Tiwari, Maya. *Women's Power to Heal: Through Inner Medicine.* Chandler, North Carolina: Wise Earth Ayurveda Ltd., 2007.

Trungpa, Chögyam. *Shambhala: The Sacred Path of the Warrior.* Boston: Shambhala, 1986.

Ullmann, Liv. *Changing.* New York: Alfred A. Knopf, 1977.

Index

About Hohm Press

Hohm Press is committed to publishing books that provide readers with alternatives to the materialistic values of the current culture, and promote self-awareness, the recognition of interdependence, and compassion. Our subject areas include parenting, transpersonal psychology, religious studies, women's studies, the arts and poetry.

Contact: Hohm Press, PO Box 4410, Chino Valley, Arizona, 86323; USA; 800-381-2700, or 928-636-3331; email: publisher@hohmpress.com

Visit our website at www.hohmpress.com

Author Contact Information

Regina Sara Ryan is a book editor, writing coach and seminar/retreat leader, and the author of eleven books, including *The Woman Awake, Feminine Wisdom for Spiritual Life*, and the classic, *Wellness Workbook* (co-authored with John Travis, M.D.) As an elder spiritual practitioner she is dedicated to passing on basic wisdom principles from numerous traditions, especially how to work with the mind and emotions. Her popular seminars and retreats have been given in the U.S., Mexico, Canada and Europe. She lives in the high desert of Paulden, Arizona with her husband of forty-four years.

Contact: www.reginasararyan.com
reginasararyan@gmail.com

Shinay Tredeau holds a BA in Humanities and Expressive Arts. A yoga instructor, yoga health coach, author and storyteller, she is dedicated to fostering intergenerational learning communities all over the world. Her writing has been featured in spiritual journals, independent magazines and online publications. She has spent the last thirteen years studying the human body through cultural immersions, dance, writing and yoga. As the wife of a wild-land firefighter, she spends summers in the high desert of Arizona, cooking delicious food and occasionally working. Her love for writing is surpassed only by her love for dancing.

Contact: www.shinaytredeau.com
shinaytredeau@gmail.com

www.womenchallengethelie.com
Contact us for a book club guide